LITTLE GIRL
LOST

INGRID STEEL

LITTLE GIRL LOST

Edited by Chris Newton

MEMOIRS

Cirencester

Published by Memoirs

MEMOIRS
PUBLISHING

Memoirs Books

25 Market Place, Cirencester, Gloucestershire, GL7 2NX
info@memoirsbooks.co.uk   www.memoirsbooks.co.uk

Copyright ©Ingrid Steel, October 2011
First published in England, October 2011
Book jacket design Ray Lipscombe

ISBN 978-1-908223-41-8

All rights reserved.

No part of this publication may be reproduced, stored in a retrieval system, or transmitted in any form or by any means, electronic, mechanical, photocopying, recording or otherwise without the prior permission of Memoirs.

Although the author and publisher have made every effort to ensure that the information in this book was correct when going to press, we do not assume and hereby disclaim any liability to any party for any loss, damage, or disruption caused by errors or omissions, whether such errors or omissions result from negligence, accident, or any other cause. The views expressed in this book are purely the author's.

Printed in England

LITTLE GIRL LOST

Contents

Chapter One	THE ORPHANAGE	1
Chapter Two	NEW FACES	21
Chapter Three	THE FARMHOUSE	34
Chapter Four	WINDSOR	52
Chapter Five	BACK TO THE ORPHANAGE	66
Chapter Six	A LITTLE HAPPINESS	74
Chapter Seven	THE CULVERS	85
Chapter Eight	HAWKRIDGE AGAIN	93
Chapter Nine	BORSTAL	106
Chapter Ten	THE MENTAL HOSPITAL	113
Chapter Eleven	CHRISTMAS IN WINDSOR	128
Chapter Twelve	THE TRUTH AT LAST	133

Acknowledgements

I am very grateful to my husband Chris for his support and encouragement during the long and difficult writing of my story. Thanks also to the man in Bromley Library for his encouragement, and to Annette Brown for proof reading and correcting grammatical errors.

My thoughts and memories from my past are summed up in this poem, written by a good friend, Annette Brown.

I wonder who I really am--
I want to know, if I ever can.
Trying to find my history,
Such a puzzle and a mystery.
My story I will piece together.
I'll not give up, I'll try forever.
So it's like the quilt I made before,
Small pieces sewed with fingers sore.
I made the colours a memory
Of all those people in my story.

Matron is the colour gold.
The special kindness which she showed,
A memory which I need to hold.
She watched me from the age of four.
I, clad in small red ankle boots
And grey bell coat, came to her door.
She nurtured me, allayed my fears,
Bathed my wounds with salty tears.
Saw me through the rough times, too,
And called me "Little Runaway".

Cook, my little dumpy friend,
At whose kitchen door I'd often end,
Sent as a punishment by my foe.
But little did they really know
She gave me treats just like a mother.
Warm, creamy yellow is her colour.

Now for Miss Burton, the colour silver.
I think she truly loved me.
She gave me a treat, a week of heaven
And restored my self esteem.

Mrs Crockett must be white.
Another angel shining bright.
Believing in me, teaching me,
About the world, not just PE

The Hornings are a little tricky.
A rainbow of colours would be fitting.
They carried the bible wherever we went,
Read passages to me as punishment.

Pop, Pop, dear old Pop.
I choose a piece when my tears stop.
Such a brave knight for me,
What colour can he be?
Like shining armour, strong and bright
Emblazoned with colours to say what's right.

Miss Gisborne, my guardian, what colour for her?
The only one with me through to the end.
Sometimes hard as a stone,
Sometimes soft as marshmallow,
A love/hate relationship bound by the law.
An 'engagement' of sorts
So, pink diamond of course!

What colours for the rest?
Those people I detest?
Some greys for the dull ones,
Red for the dangerous
And browns for the dirty or boring.
But the evil Mr Naylor
Forever I'll remember
As the darkest and blackest of black.

Lastly, the greens, for the devil's own serpent,
Slithering along in those grasses so verdant.
Mr Cadman who harmed me, worse than a knife
Gave me a stigma to last all my life.
So slowly he's sucked the blood out of me
Refusing me access to my own history.
The file held by Government, I'm not allowed,
But the secrets of Sheila will one day be told.

Chapter One

THE ORPHANAGE

Back then, my name was Sheila Williams. Date of birth June 8 1946, place unknown. Mother and father a complete blank. This is the story of my childhood. Some names have been changed, but the things that happened are all true.

My education was zero. My IQ as a young adult was equivalent to that of a five-year-old, but my memory was excellent. I could flash back to the minutest thing that happened in my life.

I cannot recall my first home, but I remember living near huge white cliffs. Where exactly is a mystery. I clearly remember being driven along by a lady in an old-fashioned black car, the sort you would see in a gangster movie. The lady explained that she was going to look after me and be my guardian and told me her name was Miss Wilson. The place she was taking me to was to be my new home, an orphanage in Hertfordshire called Hawkridge.

I was oblivious to the fact that a war had just ended and that other children were bagged and tagged and had become orphans like me.

I was four years old. Going back in time, like being hypnotised, I remember arriving at the house, which looked like a big mansion. The driveway was dark and the overhanging trees made it look very creepy.

At the front of the house there were stone statues of lions at each side of the door, the type you would expect to see in a monastery. I remember I was wearing a grey bell-shaped coat with a black velvet bow round the collar and little red ankle boots.

As we entered, we were met by the owners, Mr and Mrs Cadman.

CHAPTER 1

Mrs Cadman, who was addressed by everybody as Matron, said "Hello, Sheila" and gave me a rag doll. She introduced me to another girl and said, "This is your new friend. Her name is Sylvia Molt." It was a bit like pick-and-mix. Sylvia was much older than I was. We both had red hair, but mine was longer and I always had it in plaits. We both had freckles and blue eyes, but we were the complete opposite in character.

Matron took us to the playroom, where there were lots of other children. Sylvia had her own friends, so I just sat in a corner clutching the rag doll and looking down at the floor. I was gritting my teeth, not talking to anyone, when all of sudden a bell started ringing. It made me jump. The other children ran out of the playroom, leaving me on my own. Matron came up to me, stooped down beside me and asked: "Are you hungry, Sheila?"

I nodded my head and she took my hand, leading me to a big room with lots of tables and chairs where everybody was standing behind their chairs, ready to say grace.

Matron sat me next to her in a smaller chair, with a cushion to make me higher. After dinner Miss Wilson came to say goodbye, and I noticed that she was holding a big envelope under her arm. She ruffled my hair and said that she would come back to see me from time to time.

When she left, I didn't really know how I felt. I could not speak very well, so I kept silent. The only way I could express myself was to cry.

The next thing I remember that first day was tagging along with the matron, climbing up never-ending stairs to what she called the attic. As she unlocked the door, I noticed that it had a funny smell. There were lots of shoes, clothes and toys and Matron said to me "We will have to fix you up with some clothes." I was given a pair of lace-up shoes, which had metal studs, and some dresses, which were then labelled and marked with my name.

CHAPTER 1

After that I was taken to a bathroom with a red painted floor. It had three baths, two small and one big. My hair was washed, then searched for nits and rinsed in vinegar. After my bath, Matron put me to bed. I didn't sleep with the other kids in the dormitory, but in a small room opposite Matron's flat which was off limits to everybody else. This room was also the sick room. It was quite plain, with a bed, a sink and a toilet.

As time went by I began to join in with the other children, but I still found it hard to express myself. I could only say a very few words and when I did try to speak, I seemed to stutter.

I soon got into the routine of everyday life, but because I was only four years old, I was not expected to do chores like the other kids.

My day began by being woken at six in the morning. Matron helped me to strip my bed, turn the mattress and then make it. It was the same procedure in the dormitory for everyone else, and all the beds had to be passed by the two staff, whom we knew only as Miss and Sir. Only then were you allowed to get dressed.

Then you had to do a chore; maybe cleaning the bathroom or the landing or another day perhaps dusting, sweeping the dormitory or polishing. These chores had to be finished before the bell went off. The first bell was to tell you to down tools, wash hands or go to the toilet, then the second was the signal to go to the dining room for breakfast and stand behind your chair. You had to wait for the staff to come in before saying grace. If you asked to be excused during breakfast, you weren't allowed to return to finish your meal.

In the dining room there were seven tables with six places to each table. I sat on Matron's table, next to her. I was so glad that I did not have to sit next to Mr Cadman because he frightened me; he never called me Sheila, only "girlie". He was a tall, stout man in his fifties with grey hair and the features of a shark.

If you were late for grace on any account, you could not just barge

CHAPTER 1

in. You had to sit in the hallway until Mr Cadman called your name. If you did not have a good excuse, you had no porridge. This rule also applied at dinner and teatime.

After breakfast, the other children would get ready for school. Before going, they had to stand in a queue and one by one they were passed by Miss or Sir. I never went to school. Instead, I use to play in the playroom. If it was a nice day Miss would take me out to the grounds and leave me in a wooden play-run, locking the gate behind her.

This play-run was no ordinary playpen. It was massive and it had a miniature roundabout, slides and ropes hanging from the trees. During the morning, Matron would come out to check on me, bringing me hot orange juice and a biscuit.

Every afternoon an eccentric woman who wore half-moon glasses with a chain attached to the ends gave me speech therapy. My lesson began with her breaking up the simple words, for example, cat or dog. If I didn't respond she would peer at me over the top of her glasses, then take them off and put the ends in her mouth. Then she would pause again before pointing them at me. She became very agitated, but I was so nervous that I would get all my words jumbled up, and my stuttering got worse.

As time went by my speech did improve, but I learned new words by listening to the other children, not with help from Miss O'Grady.

By late afternoon the other children had returned from school and there would be more chores to do. No one was allowed to wear boots indoors, only sandals, and two by two, you had to go to the outhouse to clean your boots. The first thing you did was to take a blunt knife and scrape the mud off from around the studs. Then you polished them. However, if Miss or Sir, or especially Mr Cadman, found the tiniest mark, you were sent back to clean them all over again. And if your face didn't fit, you could be in that boot house all night.

At teatime the same routine applied with the two bells. After tea,

CHAPTER 1

I would be sent to the playroom while the other children had to do evening chores.

Bedtime was at seven o' clock in the evening. After I had been at the orphanage about six months, I was moved to a room in the annexe, a small building separated from the main house which was used for the girls' sleeping quarters. They put me in a single room next to the duty room where another member of staff slept.

To get to the annexe you had to walk across the main driveway, which was surrounded by woods, and on occasion bats would fly around. For this reason Mr Cadman would carry me over to my room. He would undress me and put me to bed, fold my clothes and neatly place them on to a chair next to my bed. He then gave me my rag doll, the only toy I had. I didn't like to go anywhere without it.

Underneath my room was the laundry, which was divided into two rooms. The first was the drying room, with numerous clothes lines attached to wooden poles hanging from the ceiling. Hot pipes ran along the skirting board. In the other room there were two large sinks with carbolic soap and a box of soap flakes, a scrubbing board, two copper boilers with wooden tongs, one big mangle and a stoke type boiler. At night the older girls had to do chores in the laundry and I could hear them larking around.

One night I will never forget. Shortly after the older girls had finished and had returned to the main house, a fire broke out in the drying room right underneath where I was sleeping. I remember smoke everywhere and the loud sounds of a bell constantly ringing. The sound was deafening, and I was going hysterical. I remember being shaken by Mr Cadman, who picked me up and handed me through the window to a fireman. All the other children were lined up in twos outside, waiting to be accounted for. The matron cuddled me and then took me back to the sick room where I had slept before. Afterwards a doctor came to see me and I was taken to hospital to be checked out for smoke inhalation.

CHAPTER 1

The next morning I realized that I did not have my rag doll with me. I asked where it was, only to be told that it had been burned. I was so very attached to that rag doll. It was dirty and shabby, but it was mine. I grieved for it all day, so the matron gave me a teddy, which I threw away. The cleaners were constantly picking it up and giving it back to me, but again I would throw it away. This was the first time I threw a tantrum.

That evening Matron took me to bed. I did not hold her hand, just Burtonled along behind her. Even when she tried to comfort me, I just pulled back. However, she did sit on my bed and told me a story about a man called God. She put my hands together and said "Dear God, please keep Sheila safe tonight, secure from all her fears. May angels guard her while she sleeps until morning light appears."

I asked her "Who is God?"

And she replied, "God is your father in heaven and on earth."

"What's heaven?"

"It's a place where people go to rest when they die."

"What's die?"

"It is like your doll. She's gone to heaven and God will make her nice and clean and an angel will keep her safe from any more fires."

Saturday, and only the morning chores to be done. After dinner, we would all line up for our pocket money. I only got three pennies, as I was the youngest. If you broke any crockery while doing the washing up or anything, you had to forfeit your pocket money.

After that we had to walk in a crocodile line, one member of staff at the front and other at the back, into the village. When we reached the sweet shop, only two of us were allowed in at a time. When we had returned to the orphanage, one by one we were asked to hand over our sweets, which were then put into our own personal sweet tin, with our names on, and during the week they would be rationed out. My tin always seemed to be empty.

CHAPTER 1

Continuing through to the afternoon, we had two hours' playtime when everybody had to go outside. The only exception would be if it was raining. I wasn't allowed to roam around, as the older children had to keep an eye on me.

There were acres and acres of grounds with woods, an orchard and a swimming pool, which was out of bounds unless you were escorted by a member of staff. There was also a small netball pitch and some swings. Near the swings we had some goats which were all tied up with ropes. The ropes were attached to another rope suspended between two bushes so that they could graze.

Beyond a dirt path, there were huge old chestnut trees and you could see red squirrels running along the branches. Beyond this little path was a summerhouse built on stilts, with an old thatched roof, leaded windows and a platform sticking out. This rickety old summerhouse was only used for privileges, to play table tennis, darts or shove halfpenny. It was out of bounds otherwise. Underneath it, we had about twenty rabbits in hutches and nearby was a pond with water lilies and frogs, surrounded by a rockery and tall grass. This was called the swamp, and it became a very important place for me.

We even had outside toilets so that no one had any excuses for sneaking back into the house. These toilets were also used for punishments. Come rain or shine, thunderstorm or hailstones, you were sent in the evening to the outside toilets to tear up a stack of newspaper into squares for everyone to wipe their bums. It took hours. When you had finished your hands were black, so then you had to scrub them in Gumption, which stung horribly.

Saturday teatime was different from weekdays as we had cream buns. When the staff sitting at the other end of the table were not looking, the kids would turn the plate around so the biggest cream buns were facing them. But then you had the bullies: if they saw you going to move the plate, they would kick you underneath the table, right in the shin. None of us were allowed to stretch across the table. We always had to say 'please' or 'thank you' and there was no talking unless you were spoken to by staff. If you were caught scoffing your food you would be dismissed and go without the rest of your meal.

Mr Cadman would walk around the tables in a rage and if anyone had their elbows on the table, he would clout them round the head. When everybody had finished eating, he would often stand up to reprimand someone and send them to the office for a caning. However, this time it was about the cause of the fire: someone had been smoking in the drying room and some of the clothes had caught alight.

He spoke in a normal tone at first but built himself up into a rage, shouting and banging his fist on the table. An automatic reaction would build up inside me: when I got nervous, I started laughing to the point where I could not stop. This really annoyed Mr Cadman. I would bite the inside of my mouth, as it was the only way I could stop myself laughing.

He started to say that a fire drill would have to be carried out and that the fire bell was liable to be set off at any time, night or day, and everybody would have to learn the fire code.

"If you smell smoke or see fire, tell the nearest member of staff. If you are in bed, get up quickly and quietly, get dressed and stand at the foot of your bed until a member of staff tells you what to do. When everybody has been accounted for a pillow will be placed outside the dormitory to signify that everyone is safely out."

Saturday night was 'nit' night. We had to queue up one by one to have our hair looked at and combed through with antiseptic lotion and then join another queue outside the 'red' bathroom for hair wash and a vinegar rinse. During the week, one day we had a bath, and the next day a strip wash. After a bath, we formed yet another queue for hot cocoa, but if you had wet the bed the previous night, you had to go without.

CHAPTER 1

Sunday was a day of leisure and simplicity. No chores to do, only bed making. After breakfast we would queue up for church collection money, which was one halfpenny. Then we walked in a crocodile line, with the members of staff front and back, to St Peter's Church. Everyone knew the orphan kids were coming; they could hear us, with our hobnail boots on, clattering along. The actual church service was all very confusing to me. I found it very hard to sit down for such a long time, and every time I fidgeted somebody would be 'shushing.'

After dinner, we younger ones would return to the playroom while the older children went to the lounge room, all of us for one hour's silence. There was no wireless or any recreational activities. Then the silence would be broken by the front door bell being constantly rung by the visitors and relations of the other children.

I felt bitter about having nobody to come and see me, make a fuss of me or bring me presents. And to think that I believed that God was my Father, expecting him to come and bring me wonderful things! Seeing the other children's mums and dads just made things even worse. I tried to mingle in with the other children's parents and would try to scrounge sweets from the other kids when their parents were not looking, but I just got pushed away. I was so frustrated at not being wanted that I got jealous and angry. I threw a tantrum, which got me nowhere; instead, I was given a thrashing and locked up in a small room until the visitors had gone.

At Sunday teatime, we all had to rotate to the next table. Instead of sitting on Matron's table, I was now on Mr Cadman's table, right beside him. All the other children were frightened of him as well, yet he was the one who would undress me and tuck me up in bed.

I will never forget this particular Sunday teatime. The table was set with lovely cream buns, buttered bread and strawberry jam, but first we had to eat our starters. The staff at the end of the tables had to choose one of us to serve. Yet again there was a set procedure to

CHAPTER 1

follow; you had to walk out of the dining room, round to the kitchen and stand outside until the hatch was opened by cook, then announce to her which table you were on and how many were present. I had never done it before as I was too young, but on this day Mr Cadman chose me.

As I got up I could feel my legs going all wobbly, and when I stood waiting for Cook to open the hatch, my heart began thumping. When she asked me what table I was on, I was so nervous that I couldn't answer her. I began to stutter and the other kids waiting behind me began to laugh. Cook handed me two plates with Welsh rarebit on, but as soon as she gave them to me, I dropped them.

The other kids just kept on laughing, and Cook started shouting. All hell broke out. I was kicking the other children and throwing the plates. Mr Cadman grabbed hold of me and dragged me along the floor, hitting me at the same time. I was locked up in my bedroom with nothing to eat.

I really hated Sundays. Go to church, sing and pray to a man on a cross, then the mums and dads. I was glad to go to bed and be tucked underneath the bedclothes having beautiful dreams. I realised by now that I had no real mother or father, but I could not understand why.

Year in and year out, you had to abide by the rules and regulations. I was now six and a half. My birthdays were just like any ordinary day; no party poppers or paper hats. I was given some sweets and one toy, which was secondhand, from out of the attic. I was truly grateful, especially for the sweets, but all I really wanted was be like the other kids.

As I grew older, I became resilient to orphanage life. I was more and more inquisitive, and observed everything that went on around me. I constantly asked questions and got bleak replies. I earwigged on staff conversations, which got me into trouble. In fact I was growing up distrusting everybody, including Miss Wilson, my

CHAPTER 1

guardian. She came to visit me every month, always holding a big envelope under her arm, which was actually a folder. I was curious as to what was inside that folder, so I asked her and she replied that it was a file, a story about me and about my behaviour. I asked her outright if my mum and dad were in the story, but she just changed the conversation. She told me to run along and play with the other children, who were all playing silly games like doll's house or pretending to be like mums with silly plastic cups and saucers. None of this sort of play ever appealed to me.

Getting up to mischief was more my scene. Like running after Jasmine, the boxer dog, pinching his stump of a tail then watching him going crazy, going round and round trying to bite my hand. I would also play 'he' with the boys, or even climb trees. And I always seemed to be getting caught running through the house by Mr Cadman, so again I would be punished. I had to sit in the hallway for hours and the other children would deliberately walk past me with cutting remarks, or throw things at me because they knew that I couldn't get up and walk away.

My favourite game was to sit down by the swamp; I called it my den. I would watch the tadpoles being born out of this slimy stuff and torment the frogs with a twig just to see them leap up in the air. I would lose all track of time. One day, after I had failed to hear the bells for teatime, I ran as fast as I could up to the main house, unaware of my muddy boots, as I would have to be excused for being late. I knew that the incident would not be forgotten. Mr Cadman had his beady eyes on me while I was eating my tea and I knew that he would be waiting for an opportunity to pounce on me.

When pudding was served I was gobsmacked; I couldn't believe what I was seeing. It was tapioca, and looking down at my pudding it reminded me the slimy frogspawn down at the swamp and I imagined tiny tadpoles leaping out of my dish.

CHAPTER 1

Mr Cadman was still glaring at me. He shouted, "Eat your pudding, girlie!" but I couldn't, and my nervousness made me begin to laugh. Mr Cadman was not amused. He went crazy, banging his fist on the table and shouting, all his spit flying in my face. Then he clouted me round the head. I was terrified, and laughed no more.

I was told that the swamp was out of bounds, because of snakes. "Adders have been seen round there" he said. After he had finished ranting and raving he sent me to scrub the floor, owing to my muddy boots.

As I scrubbed I started scheming. How could I run away? But I had no money and I was frightened of the dark. The more I thought of the horrible chores and being called 'girlie' or 'Williams', the more miserable and sad I felt, until tears were streaming down my face. However, as usual I got over my anguish.

After that, instead of going down to the swamp, I played with the boys climbing trees, daring each other to see who could jump from the highest branch. I would often rip my clothes, and then the older girls would bully me because they had to sew them up again. I tried to play with the other girls on the swings, but I got fed up listening to their moaning and groaning and being bitchy. All of them got up to some sort of trickery. I got so bored, just swinging, and was looking for more devilish things to get up to.

Near the swings, the goats were grazing with all the ropes tied to them. I decided to let them go free. They went running in every direction. I couldn't stop laughing and the goats seemed to be laughing too. Some were running through the woods, while others ran towards the house. I didn't know which one to try to catch first, and in the end, everyone was trying to catch them, including all the staff.

I was caned several times for that and all my privileges were stopped: no pocket money, forbidden to go out and play, and sent to bed straight after tea. And I was given extra chores to do.

CHAPTER 1

I didn't care. I had become hardened to all the beating and all the routines. It was like water off a duck's back, though deep down inside I yearned for someone to love me.

During the day I was confined to the kitchen, under Cook's orders for chores. I enjoyed being under her influence. She was small and dumpy but full of life, and when she addressed me, she always called me Sheila. Even though she gave me lots of work, like scrubbing the floor or cleaning the cutlery with Brasso, she always spoilt me by giving me a handful of sweets. When she baked cakes, I had to wash up all the utensils but she also let me lick out the cake mixture from the mixing bowl. If I worked hard, she would even let me sample the cakes.

Cook only worked until late afternoon. Before leaving, she locked the kitchen and handed over the keys to a member of staff. In the evenings I had to peel a bucket of potatoes, but first I had to report to the member of staff with the keys to take me down to the pantry and unlock the door so that I could fill my bucket with them. Next to the sack of potatoes were huge boxes of loose biscuits, and when the staff member wasn't looking I would have one hand in the potato sack and one hand in the biscuit box, stuffing biscuits up the legs of my knickers. When I had finished, the staff would lock the door and leave.

I had to go to the cold scullery to peel the potatoes, but at the same time I was scoffing the biscuits, so I didn't mind. I didn't think anyone knew I had stolen any biscuits, but the older kids had been spying on me. They threatened to either beat me up or tell on me if I did not share the biscuits with them, and told me to get more next time.

The next day, I knew in my heart that I shouldn't take any more biscuits as it was Mr Cadman who unlocked the door. My hands were shaking as I dipped into the biscuit box. My knicker legs were bulging and Mr Cadman kept on saying "Hurry up girlie, we haven't got all day". I scrambled up the steps, terrified of being caught, but then I tripped, dropping the bucket with the potatoes in and they went

CHAPTER 1

rolling down the steps. Biscuits were falling out of my knickers, but I was so nervous that I couldn't stop laughing.

Mr Cadman went bright red with anger. He kept on pushing me and shouting, "What the hell do you think you're up to girlie, stealing out of the fucking pantry!" He then pushed me again, and I lost my footing and fell down the concrete steps. I gashed my head and blood was pouring down my face. I was carried by another member of staff to the sick bay, where Matron attended to me.

Matron only had kind words, and many times when her husband had hit me I saw tears in her eyes. She cuddled me and asked me to try not to laugh when being reprimanded "Because it agitates people, which makes them angry."

Miss Wilson also came to see me. Mr Cadman had told her that I had been stealing and had tripped and fallen down the stairs. She kept staring at the gash I had on my head and had tears in her eyes. "What are we going to do with you?" she said. I replied "I want my mother and father please."

Then she asked me if I would like to go for a ride in her car. I nodded and we both got in. She threw my file on to the back seat. As we were driving along she started to make conversation. She asked me if I had enjoyed the biscuits and how many I had given away to the other kids. She also asked about the cut on my head, then after a pause said "Is it true that you tripped down the steps, or were you pushed? And I want the truth."

I replied sheepishly that I had tripped. I was too frightened to tell the truth. Miss Wilson raised her eyebrow. She knew in her heart what had happened when she saw the tears in my eyes.

By now, we had driven to Watford. Miss Wilson parked the car in a back street and we walked through the churchyard, past the graves and into Watford High Street. She explained to me that it was market day. I hated mingling with crowds, with people pushing, shoving and

CHAPTER 1

shouting. It also meant seeing pretty clothes and shiny trinkets, which made me envious.

One stall I did enjoy was the pet stall with all different kinds of animals. I tried to stroke a rabbit by poking my fingers through the wire mesh. I was one of the few who didn't have a pet rabbit at the orphanage, and to my amazement, Miss Wilson asked me if I would like to have one for myself. Of course I nodded yes.

Driving back to the orphanage, I didn't care about all the bad things. Now I had my rabbit to cuddle and to love. Miss Wilson kept looking at me every now and again and smiling. She asked me if I had thought of a name for my rabbit and I said "Snowy", because he was white.

Weeks and months passed by and I managed to stay out of trouble. I did my chores quickly so that I could be with Snowy. Cook would leave me some titbits out and Matron would give me a few extra pennies for straw.

Then Mr Cadman explained to us one teatime that everyone who had a rabbit would have to be escorted to the rabbit hutches, as a lot of adders had been seen near the swamp. The next morning a group of us were escorted down to clean out our hutches, but the gardener stopped us half way. We were told that the rabbits were sick. There was an epidemic of myxomatosis and all the rabbits would have to be destroyed. Everything was burned as we looked on from a distance. I thought to myself, first my rag doll and now my rabbit.

Cook took pity on me. She had bought me a colouring book and a box of wax crayons, so I spent some of my day sitting in the kitchen with her, not for a punishment, just for a good old chinwag and hoping a few cakes would come my way. She knew all the gossip and I knew this was my opportunity to pick her brains. I asked her sneakily: "I suppose you've seen lots of children come and go. Where do they go?"

CHAPTER 1

Cook was stunned. She told me to be like the three wise monkeys and not to keep on asking questions, because I would be none the wiser.

"But as you are so inquisitive to know everything, I'll tell you there is a new boy coming" she said. And just as she said that, the doorbell rang. I started to run out, being nosey, but the cook called me back saying, "Mr Cadman is on the warpath!" So instead I peeped from behind the door.

When I looked, I saw many people congregating in the hall. Then I saw the new boy, being smothered with lots of kisses. He looked very posh, with a knee length suit, but what tickled me pink was his little dickey-bow. He wore glasses, and when I heard him speak, he sounded very intellectual, not like me. However, I took a liking to him.

I wanted him to be my friend, so I asked him if he could keep a secret. Forgetting what Mr Cadman had said, I told him I would show him my hiding place. I took him down to the swamp and showed him my den. We picked a long piece of grass to poke the frogs with, just to see them leap, but all of a sudden, he started to squeal - "Owww!"

I thought he was just being a sissy over some stinging nettles, but something had bitten him. I got frightened and started screaming for help. In no time, staff and Matron crowded round him and an ambulance was sent for. He was taken away and never returned to the orphanage.

Mr Cadman later told us, at teatime, that the boy had fallen out of the tree, but I knew differently. Two days later bulldozers and trucks came and the swamp was concreted over.

At night, I started to have nightmares and often found myself in a wet bed in the morning, for which I was punished. One particular night I was sent off to bed early due to my bed-wetting. I was all alone in the annexe, away from the main building, and it began to get very dark, then it started to thunder. I got so frightened that I thought God was punishing me for taking that boy down to the swamp. As the lightning was flashing, I saw a shadow of a figure and started screaming.

The next thing I knew Mr Cadman was shaking me, trying to bring me to my senses, but I knew that the figure which I had seen had been him, spying on me. Or was it a figment of my own imagination? But my mind still felt that I was to blame and as Mr Cadman was shaking me he kept on saying,

"You pushed that boy out of that tree!"

I lost my appetite after that and picked at my food. The staff held me down while Mr Cadman tried to force-feed me by ramming the spoon down my throat. I struggled desperately, retching and vomiting everywhere. Matron was crying and the other children were horrified. Mr Cadman was panting in anger, shouting at the member of staff to fetch a bottle of cod liver oil.

"If you don't eat your food girlie, by God you're going to have this instead" he shouted. As he was trying to restrain me, the spoon jerked, cutting my lip. He then dragged me out of the dining room and told me to get to my bed.

All that night I tossed and turned. My stomach was making revolting noises through being hungry, and when I woke up in the morning, I felt very ill.

Matron transferred me to the sick bay, where I stayed nearly two weeks with tonsillitis. Matron explained to me that I had had a fever and the doctor had come. I was unaware that this had happened.

One bonus of being ill was having ice-cream, banana custard, blancmange and a special treat from Matron, a cream bun. And instead of having cod-liver-oil, I had a tablespoon of malt. Tasty, and I loved it!

However, I soon became bored of lying in bed. I was bursting with energy, wanting to get up to something. I hung out of the window to see if I could see the other kids, to catch up with the gossip, but I was

CHAPTER 1

caught by staff and told to get back to bed. I sneaked out of the sick bay and sat at the top of the stairs, trying to get the other kids' attention by hissing through the banisters, and again I was caught and sent back to bed.

I was annoyed at being cooped up in a small room but then I heard Matron's footsteps coming towards the door with my tea tray. Instead, she gave me my play clothes and told me to go to the dining room for my tea.

It felt good standing behind the chair saying grace again, and when we all sat down, I had a good look around to see if anybody new had come to the orphanage. I soon spotted a new girl. She was staring at me and whispering to the other girls on her table.

After tea, my friend Sylvia kept on chatting and sniggering about who had had their privileges stopped and who had had a caning. At the end of her tittle-tattle she eventually told me about the new girl, Kathleen, and how she was bullying everyone. Because she was that much older, she dared the other girls in the dormitory to do thing like running up and down the landing after the lights had gone down, and was telling ghost stories, making the other girls cry.

Kathleen ordered us to make our beds slowly to enable her to finish first and get to the washbasins before us, just so that she could look good in front of Matron, because she was on probation for her bad behaviour.

That night in the dormitory I kept a low profile, but Kathleen kept on asking me questions. Why didn't I have any parents? Had I got any brothers or sisters? Why had I been put in an orphanage? She became very persistent with her questions, so I told her that my parents had died in a car crash. Then I pulled the bedding over my head and went to sleep.

The following morning when Matron woke us up I sprang out of bed, stripped it, turned the mattress and made it. I was the first to

CHAPTER 1

finish, so Kathleen was not amused. Again that night I kept a low profile, but Kathleen started to antagonize me by making nasty comments about my parents, that they didn't want me. Then she started to sing this song, over and over again:

Once I had a mother and she was kind to me
And when I was in trouble, she sat me on her knee.
Last night as I lay dreaming upon my mother's bed
An angel came from heaven and said my mother was dead.
I woke up in the morning to see if that was true
My mother gone to heaven above the sky so blue.
Oh children obey your mothers, and do what you are told
When you lose your mother, you miss her most of all.

I tried to block her out of my mind by putting my fingers in my ears, but she was so annoying that I just exploded with anger and brutally attacked her with all my strength. Even the staff on duty had a struggle to separate us. I took the punishment, which was to stand on a chair on the landing with no shoes on and only a thin nightie. I was cold and kept snivelling over the things that she had said, until eventually Miss gave me permission to go back to bed.

The following morning again I finished making my bed first, but then Kathleen told Matron that I had not turned my mattress, even though I had. Matron felt underneath the mattress to see if it was still warm and then she asked me to strip it. "Strip it!" she repeated. I was so angry and determined not to make the bed again that I said "No!" Then Matron smacked me round the legs several times and I retaliated by kicking.

Mr Cadman was called. He shouted at me and gave me a good beating in front of the other girls. Then I was dragged along the floor,

CHAPTER 1

stripped of my clothes and locked in a spare room. I was devastated and sobbed my heart out, knowing that I had been telling the truth.

The next day I had burn marks on the tops of my legs and around my buttocks, from being dragged along the floor. Matron put dabs of calamine lotion on my legs. In her own sweet way, she always did her best to comfort me. It was not getting any easier.

Chapter Two

NEW FACES

Miss Wilson came to see me for her usual monthly visit, clutching my file underneath her arm. She spoke very harshly towards me, saying that I was becoming a problem, fighting with the other children and being disobedient. Listening to her, I felt a lump in my throat and my eyes filled with tears. I couldn't answer her as I was afraid of stuttering. It deeply hurt me, being accused of wrongdoings as a result of being bullied, and it took me a long time to get over the mental pain, longer than the physical pain.

Miss Wilson flicked through the papers in my file.

"Would you like an auntie and uncle to take you out at weekends, starting with this weekend?" she said.

I replied, snivelling,

"What do I call them?"

"You just call them Auntie and Uncle."

After she left, I leaped up into the air with joy and expectation. I started counting the seemingly endless days as they went by, and kept repeating to myself, "Please let them come." I had been told so many things that were supposed to happen but never materialized.

Finally the weekend came and I sat in my 'boudoir' dressed in my Sunday best and waiting patiently. Mr Cadman asked me to stand up for inspection. He checked my pockets, checked my shoes, and then he flicked me over the head, reminding me to behave myself and to watch my manners.

I spotted a car drawing up outside the front door and I got quite anxious, wondering if it was them. Matron answered the door and they all had an 'adult' talk before calling me over. When Matron introduced me I found that I just could not speak or express my feelings after having been so excited all week. I just nodded or shrugged my shoulders when answering.

Driving away from the orphanage, my auntie was chattering away to me, how she adored her two dogs. She said my new uncle was a doctor. As we drove up to their house, I felt agitated and kept on chewing the inside of my mouth and as we walked inside, I felt even more uncomfortable. It was like a palace, with beautiful carpets everywhere. I had only been used to wooden floors up to now. There were expensive ornaments all over the place and they asked me in a most polite manner not to touch them. Even at the dinner table, I felt the same: The knives had ornate markings on them and the china had gold trimming round the edges.

As we ate our dinner my new auntie and uncle kept on asking me questions.

"Do you like school? Do you have many friends? Do you have many toys?"

I replied in my stuttering way that my doll had been burned and died and my rabbit had been sick and had to be burned, so he died; I couldn't go to school because I couldn't speak and an eccentric lady who gave me some lessons had left because I think I had annoyed her, but that I was going to start school now.

They seemed astonished.

During the afternoon, I felt more at ease. I played with the dogs, tormenting them when no one was looking. I scoffed sweets while glued to the television. But time had slipped away so fast and this small amount of happiness had come to the end. I stood watching my auntie bagging up some sweets for me to take back to the orphanage and I had my fingers crossed behind my back, praying that I would get them before we arrived. She gave them to me as we got into the

CHAPTER 2

car and I gave a big sigh of relief. Then my uncle gave me a ten shilling note. I was so excited - nobody had ever given me any money like that.

As we drove away I looked back at the house, knowing deep in my heart that this grand house was where I wanted to live. Then I started to fill my knicker legs up with sweets, squeezing as many in as I could, with a lot of difficulty as my uncle told me not to fidget while he was driving.

When I arrived back at the orphanage they both kissed me goodbye. I wiped the kisses off, but as I waved goodbye, my eyes were filled with tears. I handed over my sweets and the ten shilling note to Mr Cadman. When he asked me if that was all the sweets I had to go into my sweet tin, I replied "Yes sir" As I went past him I walked very slowly, praying none of the sweets would fall out of my knicker legs. All the orphan kids had their own way of hiding things, which were handed down to the next lot.

By this time everyone else was in the dormitory. I had to report to Miss over at the annexe so that she could put the bolt on the door. In fact, it wasn't a bolt; it was a long steel bar which fitted into an iron slot each side. The only way anyone could sneak into our dormitory was the back way, through the downstairs flat occupied by Mr Cadman's daughter and son in-law. Mr Cadman had a key and on many occasions he would sneak up the stairs in the early hours of the morning. When Miss tuned the lights down, I could hear the other girls in the dormitory whispering "Sheila Williams is back."

I got undressed and ducked underneath my bed clothes, took all the sweets out of my knickers and counted them, knowing just how many I could give away. I shared them out but kept more for myself. I bragged about my auntie and uncle, saying they were going to be my new mother and father and that I was going to live in a grand house.

CHAPTER 2

This same thing happened each weekend for the next four weeks and all this time I was in a daydream, dreaming all kinds of things. Matron even trusted me to go up to the local post office on my own to buy Premium Bonds. She gave me an envelope with my money in it, the money that my uncle had given me over the past weeks. I handed over the envelope to the postmaster and when he gave it back, he had put a receipt inside. I asked him if the receipt and the Premium Bonds had my name on them, and could I have a look at my name please. I knew I could not read, but the name Sheila Williams was written on a label inside all my clothes, so if I saw the name, I would recognise it straight away.

The postmaster was a bit confused, knowing that I was an orphan who stood in the crocodile line each week queuing up at the sweet counter. But I was no-one's fool, nor was I a dunce. He showed me my name, so I knew everything was hunkydory.

When I took the envelope back to Matron, she remarked, "If your Premium Bonds come up you'll be a rich little girl!" I just kept on praying, each week to see my auntie and uncle.

The next week was extra special. My uncle drove us to a historical place with huge stone blocks all mounted in different ways and different shapes and sizes. There was an old wishing well, so I kept on asking my uncle for pennies to throw down it. Not to wish for anything; just to hear the echoing sounds. Afterwards we all sat down on the grass to have a picnic and while we were eating, I asked them if they were my real mother and father. They both stopped eating, amazed at what I had said.

"No" said my aunt. "We both wanted to make you happy by being your friend and taking you out. We have invited you into our home and given you pennies for the wishing well."

There was a short silence. I suppose I had taken them unawares, and they were shocked at what I had said. Anyway, we carried on

CHAPTER 2

with our picnic. We played 'hi' round the huge stone blocks and I did some cartwheels and roly-polys down the hill.

Then we went back to their home for tea and my auntie bagged up some sweets as usual before taking me back to the orphanage. I went through the same procedure as usual when I got back to the orphanage and told the same story. I elaborated on all the good things which were going to happen to me when I left the orphanage for good with my new mother and father.

The following week I was all dressed up in my glamorous Sunday best, the same old clothes and my hobnail boots. I sat in the grand hallway waiting for my auntie and uncle's car to pull up. But they didn't come. I kept looking at the clock: one hour went past, then another hour, and still no auntie or uncle.

The first bell went off, then the second bell, and all the other kids were walking to the dining room for dinner. As they walked past me, they were teasing me. "Where're your new mum and dad and your grand house now, Williams?"

Then Mr Cadman came out of the dining room.

"Take off your coat and get you into the dining room!" he shouted.

I was devastated. I ran into the cloakroom and in a rage of frustration, I pulled all the other kids' coats of the hooks and threw them into the middle of the floor in one big heap. I heard Mr Cadman shouting as he was walking towards me, so I ran for dear life. I ran as fast as I could up the driveway to the woods, then flaked out near the bushes and cried myself to sleep.

The gardener woke me up, and he was quite adamant about taking me back. But I insisted that I didn't want to go back to be punished. "Mr Cadman all my clothes off and I'm left in a locked room all day" I said. He was lost for words, but he still kept trying to sweet-talk me into going back. Eventually he talked me round and walked me back to the main house.

CHAPTER 2

I was not punished. It was the opposite; everyone was fine towards me. However, I stayed quiet for days. It was my own way of trying to come to terms with my anger and pain. In this situation, you had to get over it yourself. Something would always happen to bring me round in the end.

My seventh birthday was coming up and it seemed that a multitude of things had happened. My guardian was retiring, and on her monthly visit, she had introduced me to my new guardian, Miss Gisborne. But Miss Wilson had been with me from the age of four. She had watched over me from the beginning, through all the highs and lows. She knew precisely what went on in that orphanage. She knew that the gash on my head and all the bruises and burn marks weren't a coincidence, but that there was always an excuse behind the explanation.

My new guardian, Miss Gisborne, was very different in every way. She was much younger, and she was tall with dark brown hair. And there was not a hair out of place. She wore big glasses and had a particular habit of using her finger to push them up the bridge of her nose. She always spoke in a direct way. Now she had my story, the 'file'.

My birthday finally arrived. I expected it to be like every other birthday, with no fun or excitement. It was the week of the Coronation, though I was oblivious to what this meant and what people were doing in the outside world.

I waited patiently for the second bell to go off so that I could dash into the dining room to see how many presents I had, but Matron stood at the dining room entrance and stopped us all. We were all given paper hats in blue, red or white, and as we walked into the dining room we saw that all the tables were covered with white sheets and decorative paper cups and plates had been put out. All the tables had been joined together and our names were written in places round the table.

CHAPTER 2

My name was next to Matron's place. I was amazed at the number of presents and birthday cards in front of me. After saying grace, Matron helped me to open them all. The first present I opened was from my favourite person, Cook. She had brought me my own sweet tin filled with an assortment of sweets. The second present, when I opened it I was somewhat confused; it was brown and leathery with a brown lace and looked like a shoe Matron was laughing - she knew exactly what it was. When she took it out of the box, I realised it was a leather football which the gardener and all the staff had given me, because they were so fed up with me fighting with the boys over their ball. Then one of the staff spoke up.

"Sheila, you can stay out all day and all night, playing net ball and bouncing that ball."

"As long as she don't bounce it on my kitchen wall!" said Cook.

The next one was a joint present was from Miss Wilson and Miss Gisborne. It was a new Sunday dress. I also got an assortment of toys from the local police station's orphan box. I was overwhelmed with all my presents.

Then Cook brought in my birthday cake. I had never seen such a big cake before and it was absolutely beautiful. On top was a solid silver horse-drawn carriage.

Matron and Mr Cadman gave me a Coronation picture book. One of the pictures in it has stayed in my mind forever: the young Queen in a blue cloak and a little tiara.

Matron lit the seven candles, and as I blew them out she told me to wish for something. I wished I could have my mother and father. I could feel my lips quivering and my eyes filling with tears.

I was then made waitress. Matron cut the cake into slivers and put them on a silver tray for me to take round, giving all the kids and staff a piece. While this was going on everyone sang Happy Birthday. I was more concerned in case there wasn't enough cake left for me.

CHAPTER 2

Then Matron took the solid silver horse-drawn carriage and said, "This is yours Sheila, it belongs to you and when you are older you may have it."

The carriage was put on the mantelpiece in front of the clock in the staff sitting-room, and it was still there when I was fifteen. I will never forget that birthday for the rest of my life.

Another day and a brand new year. Now seven, and I was starting school for the first time. I had to walk to school along a winding lane, past St Peter's Church, down a hill, then past the police station and the school was round the back.

I did not have to go on my own. A new boy named Andy was coming to the orphanage, and he was going to be my chaperone. He was short and dumpy with wavy brown hair. We became inseparable and sat together in the classroom. Andy very sweetly did some of my schoolwork for me, and he was my little bodyguard in the playground. We became known as troublemakers, though. We played 'knock down ginger' on the way to school and if we saw any bicycles or scooters in peoples' gardens, we would go and nick them and take them to the police station, to our local bobbies. If they weren't claimed, they would be ours.

"Did you find them Sheila, or did you nick them?" they would say. They all knew me and every year, at Christmas, they would buy me a present out of the orphan funds. Andy would mouth off that we had found them. We had to make a statement and put our names on the dotted line and were told that if the property was not claimed within fourteen days, they would be ours to keep.

They were always claimed by their owners. We never got our hands on any of those bicycles and scooters again, but we did see them all eventually, back in their owners' gardens.

Every Sunday Andy and I went to church together and sat next to each other in the pew; we would put our donation of a halfpenny in the collection bag, but at the same time we would take out a threepenny bit and a sixpenny piece for our thanksgiving. We would hide the money until we went to school, then spend it in the sweet shop. We carried on doing this for months on end. We became such nuisances that we were made to go to Sunday school in the afternoon.

In the end, we were both caught. We waited outside Mr Cadman's office for a caning and from then onwards our pockets were sewn up. Even so, Sunday was a good day, because Andy never had anyone to come and visit him either.

There was one incident I remember when Andy and I were both in Sunday school. Andy was called up on to the stage to do some rehearsing and I was left by myself. A girl standing behind me who kept on digging me in the back. In the end I was so frustrated that I exploded in a rage. I turned round and lunged right at her. When the Sunday school teacher noticed us fighting, she immediately blamed me and called me a nasty little thing. I was so livid that I got hold of the teacher's dress and ripped it to shreds.

She was enraged. She immediately put her coat, pulled me by my shoulders and dragged me back to the orphanage. Andy was running behind us shouting "Leave her alone!"

Mr Cadman hesitantly walked towards us, but I was trying to struggle from the grip of the Sunday school teacher, so he hit me. I tried to duck but the force of the blow caught my nose and there was blood everywhere, all down my dress. As I ran away, the blood was mixed with mucus from the crying.

When I realised no one was chasing me any more I sat down in the bushes. The gardener had spotted me. He took pity on me and gave me his handkerchief. Then we both heard a noise and when the gardener went to look, he spotted Mr Cadman.

"You'd better watch out Sheila, Mr Cadman is coming!" said the gardener. I could hear Mr Cadman getting nearer and calling. "Where are you Sheila, where are you?"

CHAPTER 2

Then I spotted Andy behind Mr Cadman with a stick in his hand. I was frightened of what he might do, so I came out of the bushes. Matron came towards me and took me under her wing. She bathed my nose and took me to the attic to give me a brand new doll and some sweeties. I tried desperately to explain to Matron what had happened, but my nose had swelled up and it was hard to breath. I was shattered and fed up, always taking the blame for somebody else's bad deeds.

Soon after that Andy left the orphanage. He had only been there for respite care while his father was in prison. As he was leaving, I hid behind a tree. I was crying as I watched him go into the distance.

I missed my friend so much. I saw other children come and go. After Kathleen and Sylvia went I had been there the longest. Each time Miss Gisborne came to see me my file had got bigger and fatter.

On one occasion when she came, she tried to explain that it was time for me to be a part of a family and be fostered. When she mentioned this, my brain clicked back to the sad memories and disappointment with the auntie and uncle.

I started answering Miss Gisborne back. We had never really bonded and I found myself stuttering again. She explained some details. There would be another boy living there, so I would not be on my own. It was a large farm cottage with cats, dogs and horses which were privately owned. When I remarked that I wasn't going to call them auntie and uncle, she just sighed and told me to call them what I felt like.

I got up. "I am not going to call them mum and dad, they're not my real mother and father!" I stuttered.

When she had left I did not leap up in the air with excitement or constantly pray for my new foster parents to visit me, not this time. Nor did I go round bragging to the other kids. I still felt very insecure after the other 'auntie and uncle' experience. As I lay in bed, I did

CHAPTER 2

try to imagine the farm and what the other boy would look like. But I had to wait for a Sunday to meet my new substitute mother, father, and brother.

Every day I carried on merrily doing my chores, skipping to and from school, queuing up for my pocket money, trailing on the end of the crocodile line to the sweet shop and going to church in hobnailed boots on Sundays, to be told by the congregation, "Hush - tiptoe!"

Eventually Sunday afternoon came round and visiting time. I went through the same procedure; being passed by Mr Cadman then sitting in the hallway swinging my legs nervously while waiting for these people to arrive. When they did, I watched them all getting out of their car. They were certainly different from the auntie and uncle! Even the car looked a monstrosity, and the people looked like hillbillies.

They were called the Naylors. Matron introduced herself to them and escorted them to the interview room. This was the same room I was usually locked in for misbehaving in front of other visitors. They had a long discussion, and then I was called in and sat between Matron and Mrs Naylor. Mr Naylor and their son sat opposite and I felt all eyes were on me, which made me nervous. Mrs Naylor introduced herself as Ann, Mr Naylor as Fred and the son as Paul. They all just said hello.

Mrs Naylor did most of the talking. She was quite adamant about how she would mould me to suit herself.

"If you don't wish to call us Mother and Father, Ann and Fred will do" she said.

She took my hand, but I immediately pulled it away. Matron frowned at me and told me to run along.

I was most disappointed that the Naylors never even took me out or brought me any sweets. The visits continued for several weeks and I began to get quite impatient and bad-tempered with everyone because I did not know whether the Naylors wanted me or not. Each visiting time they told me about the farm. I heard how everyday a steam train would go by, blowing its whistle before going underneath the bridge, and lots of horses grazed in the field. Thinking about all these things and not seeing them was making me frustrated.

Miss Gisborne came to see me, yet again holding the file underneath her arm.

"Well, Sheila, how do you like the Naylors?" she asked me.

"All right" I answered.

"I would like you to settle down with a family of your own and the Naylors would like to give you that home. I'll come to see you from time to time." She added that the grandfather was also living there.

"The Naylors have had a pantry converted into a bedroom because he has to use walking sticks. They would like you to call him Pop. The Naylors felt it would be better if I told you. Under no circumstances must you torment or be rude to him, do I make myself clear, Sheila?"

"Yes Miss."

The following week I was yet again sitting in the hallway, packed and ready to leave and waiting for the Naylors to pick me up. While I was waiting the other kids kept on running past, sniggering and provoking me.

"Ha ha, Williams is leaving!" they called.

I felt like getting up to give them a good bashing, but I had to control myself. Then Cook came up to me. She kissed me on the cheek, pushed a bag into my hand and told me to be good. As she walked away, I had tears in my eyes. When I looked into the bag, I saw that she had cooked my favourite cakes. And to think that every time I was sent to her kitchen it was supposed to be a punishment. Little did they know how fond I was of the dumpy little cook.

The Naylors had now arrived and Matron called me over. She too

CHAPTER 2

kissed me, patted me on the head and told me to be good. Mr Cadman reminded me about my manners.

"Remember your temper, girly!" he said as we walked to the car.

Chapter Three

THE FARMHOUSE

As we drove to the farm down an unmade road with no street lights, it was just as the Naylors had described it. Mr Naylor drove past the cottage to the entrance to a field and asked me if I would like to go and open the gate. "Yes sir!" I replied.

He drove through, then asked me to shut the gate and stand on the running board at the side of the car. I was clutching on to the door as we drove round the field to the back entrance of the cottage. He asked me if that was fun and again I replied, "Yes sir."

Mrs Naylor showed me round the cottage. There was no bathroom, only a tin bath that was hanging outside in the yard. The only toilet was in the yard too. There was no running hot water either, just an old copper boiler. In the parlour room stood a black-leaded fireplace with pots and pans hanging on either side.

Beside the fireplace were two armchairs, one of which I remember was big and bulky and covered with a shabby-looking blanket. Mrs Naylor remarked that the chair was only for Pop.

I was led through to another room and as we walked passed a large wooden door I can clearly recall a funny smell. Mrs Naylor told me that this was the door to Pop's bedroom.

We continued into a much more pleasant room which Mrs Naylor described as the 'best room'. It had an old three-piece suite and an antique dresser. Going through yet another door, leading upstairs, she showed me Paul's bedroom, which was grossly untidy, and their room, which was large and drab. Finally, we arrived at my room, which was small but cosy. It also had the best view, overlooking the unmade road and the fields where the horses were.

CHAPTER 3

Everything was so different from what I had been used to. Even opening the doors - I kept on trying to turn a knob but they all had metal latches. Going to the toilet at night meant using a bucket left on the landing. In the orphanage we always had the landing light left on at night. I was so desperately frightened of the dark that Mrs Naylor compromised with a minute candle.

It look several months for me to settle down, and it was trial and error all round. I had to start a new school, which I did not relish because my IQ was not very high. I found myself fighting with other children who poked fun at me.

Mrs Naylor drew up a cleaning rota for Paul and me. One day Paul washed up and I dried the dishes, then at the weekend Paul had to black-lead the fireplace and I had to polish the house throughout. Paul had to clean and tidy the back yard while I had to do the Brasso, and vice-versa. Only when all of the cleaning was completed would Mr Naylor give us our pocket money. Paul was that much older than I was and he always took his money and went out with his best friend, Colin, and I was left looking like a sissy to them.

Every day Pop hobbled eight paces from his bedroom to his scruffy old armchair, where he would sit all day with his pipe glued to his mouth. Mr Naylor never said much to me, only in passing. He was always out in the garden tending to his vegetable patch or going to the park to work on the watercress beds. Mrs Naylor had a daily cleaning job for an elderly woman.

I was not used to being left on my own, so I had to learn to find ways of amusing myself. One day I decided to do some baking. I took a baking tray out of the oven into the garden and made twelve mud cakes, then I put them back into the oven ready for Mrs Naylor to arrive home. I had forgotten about the cakes but, later, when Mrs Naylor opened the oven door worms were crawling everywhere. I was immediately sent to my bedroom.

CHAPTER 3

I asked the Naylors many times if I could ride the horses and each time I was given a firm 'no'. Each day I would sit on the fence giving them titbits, and I had a burning desire to jump on their backs. The farmer must have been watching me, because he put a great big padlock on the gate. In the end, I decided to walk up the lane to the gypsies who lived there and told them that if they let me ride one of their horses, the Naylors and old man Johnson, the farmer, would give them bags and bags of rags.

It was a terrific feeling being on the back of a horse, riding along the little lanes and through the fields. It was absolutely sensational. Every day I was up there with the gypsies.

In the evenings we would all sit down and Mrs Naylor would cut a big crusty loaf of bread to go with delicious pea soup. We would all listen to The Archers on the wireless.

One evening, all of a sudden, there was a loud noise; someone was knocking at the front door. It was the gypsies and farmer Johnson. The gypsies had come for the bags of rags and the farmer had come to complain, so a big row broke out between them all. I never saw the gypsies again.

I was constantly in trouble with Mrs Naylor. At one stage she even got Mr Naylor to nail the window closed in my bedroom, because every time I saw a train coming I would jump out of the window and run up the lane before the driver blew his horn. If I ran downstairs Pop would always be in the way, so I would miss the damn train. Also, she complained all the time about me smelling of smoke from the trains.

At school, I was soon in disgrace. I was disciplined for stealing from a particular girl in my class. I detested her because she was brainy, bright and cocky with it, especially towards me because she knew that I was not as intelligent as she was, and I did not have pretty clothes.

Each morning she presented the teacher with freshly-cut flowers from her garden and the teacher seemed to give her special privileges. So one day on the way to school I decided to pick some flowers for the teacher from someone's garden. I hopped over the fence and helped myself, but little did I know that the lady of the house was watching me and reported me to the headmaster.

That night as I lay in bed I could hear the Naylors constantly arguing over whether or not to send me back to the orphanage. Then to top that, the following day I was in serious trouble again. It was Saturday morning and my turn to wash the dishes, but because Paul wanted to go out quickly, he decided that he was going to wash and leave me to dry them. Instead, we both began arguing. Pop starting shouting at us, then I started shouting at Paul that I was going to tell Mrs Naylor. But when I said that, he turned round.

"Mrs Naylor is not your mother and we don't want you living with us! Got it?" he said.

I saw red. I got the spoon I was about to dry and stabbed it into Paul's chest. There was blood everywhere. Mr Naylor happened to walk in at that very moment. Paul had passed out, so he called for an ambulance.

I stayed in my room all day with the door locked. I was terrified of the consequence what I had done and was thinking the worst, that Paul was going to die. Then I heard cars pulling up outside. The Naylors had returned and the other car belonged to Miss Gisborne, my guardian.

I immediately put my ear to the floor, trying to eavesdrop on what they were saying. I overheard Pop saying that Paul had been provoking me and telling Miss Gisborne what he had said. Mrs Naylor asked Miss Gisborne if I could go back to the orphanage, but Mr Naylor asked if I could have a second chance and that he would take all responsibility. Then they all agreed I was to be given a second chance and it was suggested that it would be a good idea if I were

CHAPTER 3

given the name of Naylor, to be equal with Paul.

Mr Naylor unlocked the door of my bedroom and told me to go downstairs. The first thing Miss Gisborne said to me was, "Have you been eavesdropping, Sheila?"

"Yes miss" I replied.

"What possessed you to do such a thing?"

I did not answer. I just stared at the floor.

"Well, the Naylors have decided to give you another chance and, thank God, Paul is going to be all right."

Life became tolerable where Paul was concerned once they had told us both that Mrs Naylor was not his real mother. She had adopted him because she could not have any children of her own.

Miss Gisborne started to visit more regularly and Mrs Naylor would tell her the ins and outs of everything that went on. Firstly she had to tell me I had been stealing Paul's pocket money and second that I was sneaking out of the house wearing other girls' clothes to school. I explained to my guardian that Mrs Naylor was altering her own clothes for me to wear, which looked horrible, and I was being teased about them at school. I also told her that Paul was always given more pocket money than I was.

Miss Gisborne then took it upon herself to issue me with pocket money each week. She also organised a trip to London for me to buy some new clothes, using my allowance which was being given to Mrs Naylor, which she had not been using.

Miss Gisborne gave me two extra treats on our trip to London. She took me to a proper photographer's shop, with fancy lights and everything, to have my picture taken and then we went to see Pollyanna at the cinema. It was a film about an orphan like me, but she was a happy orphan - not like me. All I wanted was my own family, a mother I could call Mother. The photograph of me with my gingery plaits, in my best jumper and pleated skirt with straps, was always afterwards kept on the lounge mantelpiece next to my Coronation carriage.

On one particular visit, my guardian told me something that was the greatest emotional shock of my life. She explained to me and the rest of the family that during her enquiries about changing my name to Naylor she had discovered that Sheila was not my real name.

"Your real name is Ingrid Williams" she said. "Now it will be Ingrid Naylor as suggested before."

I was very shaken by this news. It made me sad to know that I had been living for nearly ten years with the name Sheila and that if they knew my name was Ingrid they must know my mother and father. It must be in that book called the file. However, it was the thought of going to school with a completely different name - and not being able to spell it - that gave me more concern at the time.

The next day the Naylors took me to school and explained about my name both to my teacher and to the headmaster. Then he explained to the other children in my class. He also warned them that if anyone was caught sniggering or being nasty to me they would be punished. But they did poke fun at me behind the teacher's back because I couldn't even spell my own name. I kept on getting Ingrid mixed up with England.

Fortunately I managed to clear that hurdle with flying colours. Each night before going to bed Mr Naylor sat down with me and helped me to spell my name, over and over again, until I eventually got it right - not just being able to write it properly but to memorise it as well.

The only lesson I loved was PE, and I was in the gymnastics team. I could climb ropes, swinging from one to another like a monkey. I could run and jump on to the springboard and over the vault. On the beam, I could balance on one leg, do flicks, stretch my leg out as if I was a ballerina and do the splits. I was chosen to be in a gymnastics show, not because I was an orphan kid, but because I was the best. My PE teacher wanted me to jump from the springboard and over the vault through a hoop which was going to be on fire.

On Saturdays, instead of leaving me in the house to get up to mischief, Mr Naylor would take me down to the watercress beds. He also gave me a small plot in the garden so I could grow my own flowers instead of stealing them from other people's gardens.

On Sunday mornings he would call me to snuggle into their bed with them. I used to slide down between him and Mrs Naylor. I enjoyed this, though I made it quite clear from the beginning that kissing, cuddling or sitting on anyone's lap was out of the question.

A few months after I had moved in with the Naylors I started to go to Brownies. I used to meet the other girls at the council estate and we would walk together to the church hall. Mr Naylor used to meet me afterwards at the top of the unmade road, as it was pitch dark and there were no street lights. He would give me a piggy-back ride, pretending to be a horse, jogging up and down.

On one occasion I felt his hand on my vagina. I was frightened and felt uneasy so I kept on asking to get down. After this I asked Mrs Naylor to collect me, which she did religiously.

In the early evening I would look out of my bedroom window, peering into the distance for Mr Naylor to come home. When I spotted his car I would run vigorously up the lane to meet him. I would jump on to the running board on the side of the car, holding on to the door with one hand and waving my other leg and hand shouting, "Ho ha!" It was great fun. Mr Naylor and I were inseparable then, like two peas in a pod.

If I saw Mr Johnson, the farmer, with his carthorse, I would run as hard as I could, shouting, "Please let me have a ride!" My tenth birthday was on my mind, and I kept on reminding everyone, "It's my birthday soon!" In bed at night I would dream of a beautiful white pony and kept on praying to my real father in heaven that my dream would come true. Nearer the time, I became obsessed with the idea and kept on dropping hints, but they were all ignored.

My special day came at last and I was overwhelmed with excitement. I could not sit still during breakfast and I was all fingers and thumbs opening my birthday cards. Mr Naylor put a blindfold over my face and Mrs Naylor walked me through to the back door and opened it. Mr Naylor kept on twirling me round and round, and then they removed the blindfold.

I was gobsmacked, mortified and heartbroken. It was not a pony as I had imagined. Instead it was a clapped-out bicycle which appeared to have been made from spare parts collected from a rubbish dump.

I ran as fast as I could up to the little railway bridge, sobbing my heart out. I was heartbroken. After I came back to the house, each time I passed the bike I put my hand over the side of my face so that I didn't have to see it. I had no intention of riding that boneshaker.

That weekend everyone was doing their own business. Mrs Naylor went to work, Paul went out with his friend and Mr Naylor went to the watercress beds. He did not take me. I was left on my own; I had been sent to Coventry.

I sat opposite Pop, staring into his face and thinking what a disgusting-smelling old chair he was sitting in. He started to get annoyed with me. He tapped his pipe on the side of the fireplace in a temper.

"Why are you staring at me?" he said.

I didn't answer. I just kept on staring. Then he started shouting at me.

"Do you realise you are an ungrateful little missy? It took Mr Naylor a long time to make that bike."

I got up from the chair and shouted back.

CHAPTER 3

"And you are a dirty old man, sitting in that chair pissing your pants!"

I ran out of the house up to the little railway bridge. As I was leaning over the bridge gazing at the track, I heard a noise. I turned round to see Pop walking with his crutches, shouting and waving one of them at me.

Then all of a sudden, he fell to the ground. I ran down that road so fast when I saw Pop lying there with his head bleeding. I was horrified, thinking Pop was going to die. Without hesitating, I got on that bike and rode as fast as I could. The handlebars were swaying and I was weaving all over the place. When I put the brakes on by mistake, I went flying, cutting my legs and hands. Then the chain came off.

By now I had started to panic and was screaming for help. When I reached the council houses, I knocked at everyone's door, going berserk.

One woman came out and tried to calm me down. I was now hysterical. I could hardly get my words out.

"Pop dying! He lying in the road!" I stuttered.

The woman phoned for an ambulance immediately and told me to stay in the house while she got into her car to attend to Pop. I sat alone, just praying "Please God, do not let Pop die."

Then I heard the ambulance sirens going past. When the woman returned I burst into tears. She bathed my cuts, assuring me that Pop was going to be all right. She also told me she had informed the police, so they could get in touch with the Naylors.

When she said that, my stomach rolled over. I was biting the inside of my mouth, I was so nervous, knowing I could be locked away somewhere for provoking Pop.

Late in the afternoon, when the Naylors and Paul had returned from the hospital, the woman walked me home. I saw my bike was

CHAPTER 3

lying in the ditch all buckled up. As soon as I got home and the woman had said her goodbyes the Naylors started on me, asking me if I had pushed Pop over, because he never walked beyond the gate. Then Paul had a go.

"You fucking pushed that old man over didn't you?" he said.

"I did NOT push Pop over!" I said. No one believed me, but I knew in my heart that I had been the cause of Pop's fall.

"The truth will be revealed when I go to see Pop in hospital tomorrow" said Mrs Naylor. "I'll ask him what really happened."

The next day at school I kept silent, thinking about what Pop was going to say. I kept on asking the teacher if I could be excused from the classroom to go to the toilet, just to pray for Pop.

When I got home from school, I was expecting my case to be packed. I thought I would be sent back to the orphanage or locked away, but when I walked through the door Mrs Naylor was baking a cake, which meant it must be a special occasion. Mr Naylor had mended my bike and Paul had bought me a new bell for it, as the old one had been broken.

To my amazement, Pop had told the Naylors that I was the angel who had saved him.

When Pop came home from the hospital and no one was around, I gave Pop a peck on his bald head and whispered in his ear, tears streaming from my eyes. "I'm so sorry for being rude" I said.

I truly loved that old man in his smelly old chair. He had stuck up for me so many times.

Every day after that I rode that bike. I was happy as a sandboy, riding up and down the unmade road, bouncing my bottom up and down on the saddle and pretending it was a horse. I even ventured out further, riding round the council houses. I didn't care about the kids from the estate calling me names, laughing and taking the mickey out of my clapped-out bicycle made from bits from the rubbish dump.

CHAPTER 3

I was at the age when I could see danger, but the only things I was petrified of were the dark, and snakes slithering through the grass. Those two things represented the devil.

Now Mr Naylor became the devil's own demon. He started to terrorise me, knowing I was vulnerable. Nowhere to go, no one to tell, no one to believe what I said. Whenever I was in trouble, I was constantly being reminded, "You'll be locked away!"

Mr Naylor had begun to sexually abuse me. He would be lurking in the bushes with his privates hanging out and when I passed he would call me to go over to him. I deliberately misbehaved at Brownies, knowing I would be expelled, so that no one would have to meet me at the end of the unmade road and give me piggy-back rides with wandering hands.

The anxiety made me go off my food. I could not eat my dinners at school and was so hungry that I fainted while I was on the beam in gymnastics class. I was taken to the accident and emergency department at the Police Memorial Hospital at Watford. Miss Gisborne, Mrs Naylor and my teacher were all there, and I overheard Mrs Naylor say that I had started to wet the bed. They came to the conclusion that I was going down with tonsillitis. After that, Mr Naylor had left me alone.

Unknown to me, Mrs Naylor and Miss Gisborne were organising a surprise holiday - a week in Devon. Mrs Naylor had already made arrangements for Pop to go to the hospital, right next to Watford football stadium in Vicarage Road, for respite care. Mrs Naylor eventually let the cat out of the bag that 'we're all going on a summer holiday for a week or two', and I was stunned. I had thought something might be about to happen, with all the chit-chat going on. I wasn't exactly over the moon with excitement, knowing Mr Naylor was going, but seeing the blue sea and the golden sands, the ice creams and donkey rides would bring a little bit of happiness into my life.

CHAPTER 3

Pop gave me a handful of loose change before I went to the hospital and told me to be good. The night before leaving we packed the car and when it was first light and you could hear the cock crowing, we were on our way to Devon.

I was still under the weather, so I wrapped myself up with the car blanket and went to sleep. That way, I didn't have to speak to anyone, especially Mr Naylor. We stopped half way and had a bite to eat, then carried on with our journey. It was only when Mrs Naylor said "Look Ingrid! We are nearly there" that I started to get that happy feeling inside. We pulled up in a massive caravan park, packed with people.

That day we just relaxed and wandered about. I mixed in with some other kids playing hide and seek. The next day we all went down to the beach and took a picnic, and Mrs Naylor asked if I was all right. "You're exceptionally quiet" she said.

I didn't answer her; I just twiddled with the sand. I didn't feel very well. I felt cold and all I wanted to do was to go to sleep. When Mr Naylor spoke to me, I got up and went near the sea and mingled with the crowds on the beach.

That is all I can remember. I must have passed out. When I eventually came round, I was in pain and could see blisters down one side of my body. Mrs Naylor tried to explain to me that I had gone wandering off. "We found you sleeping on the beach and some people helped us to get you back to the caravan. When the doctor came, he thought you were suffering with sun stroke at first, but it's tonsillitis."

So I only saw the seaside for two days. When I was better, we all had to return to the farm.

Because I hadn't had a proper holiday the Naylors took me on another outing, which was most illuminating. I was ecstatic with excitement. We drove to the outskirts of London somewhere, a place that looked like the seaside. In fact, it was a big river with a man-made beach. There were boats and people swimming, and there was an ice-cream parlour.

CHAPTER 3

There was something about the man making the candyfloss that intrigued me greatly. I was mesmerised by him. I had a strange feeling that he was going to feature in my life somewhere. He asked if I wanted one and I replied "I don't have any money, sir."

"This is especially for you" he said, looking me in the eye and handing me some candyfloss. I thanked him and made my way back to the Naylors, very slowly, making a pig of myself eating that candyfloss. It was so sticky, and I was soon in a right mess. It was all over my swimming costume.

When I got back I was surprised to see only Mr Naylor there, so I sat down as far away from him as I could. He told me to take my swimming costume off because it was attracting the wasps. I instantly shouted back to him, "No, I am not taking nothing off! Got it?"

Mr Naylor got up in a rage and pulled at my swimming costume in front of all the people on that beach. My stomach was turning over, but I managed to free myself and I ran away as fast as I could. I had to go to the Ladies, but I got there too late and had an accident in the toilet.

I was in a right state. I tried to wash my swimming costume down the toilet and kept on flushing the toilet with water and I tried to clean my legs with the horrible toilet roll.

There were people constantly in and out of the toilets and I was in there naked for hours. I could hear my name being called on the loud speaker, then I heard some women saying in a conversation, "There is a little girl gone missing the police have been informed."

Eventually the toilets went quiet and I burst into tears. I was now in big trouble. When I heard footsteps, I opened the door and asked the lady if she could help me. She became all flustered and told me to stay while she went to get some help, which she did. Some women helped me, and Mrs Naylor was there too. There was no excitement that I had been found, but she just looked at me and frowned. The police officer bent over and asked if I was all right

CHAPTER 3

"Did you have a bad stomach ache and was you afraid to come out of the toilet?"

"Yes miss" I lied.

On the way back to the farm Mrs Naylor asked what had happened to me. I told her I had a pain in my tummy. If I had told her the truth I would have been called a liar, so I just kept my mouth shut as usual.

In the end, Pop caught Mr Naylor in the act of trying to abuse me in the toilet while Mrs Naylor was in the bath. I was locked in my bedroom, being manipulated by the family. I was trembling in fear waiting for my guardian and a woman from the authorities to come to take me back to the orphanage.

Leaving the Naylors was horrendous. I waited in my locked room with the windows nailed down for my guardian to collect me. All I could hear was Mrs Naylor going hysterical and screaming. Mr Naylor was banging furniture around, Pop was shouting and Paul was slamming all the doors on his way out. Then he started to throw stones at my window.

I felt weak and kept going dizzy. I hadn't eaten a proper dinner for ages - I had given most of them to the dog when Mrs Naylor wasn't looking. I had no fight left in me and I was sobbing my heart out, trembling in fear.

I heard cars pulling up and when I looked out of the window, I saw a police car. I was petrified and found it hard to breathe with the anxiety. Miss Gisborne unlocked my door and put a blanket round me. The police officer helped her to escort me downstairs and round the back way, away from the Naylors, to the car. There was another woman there, from the Authority.

Miss Gisborne helped me to lie down in the back of her car and the woman from the Authority escorted us back to Hawkridge. Matron took me to the sick bay, which was opposite her flat. The next few days, each time I tried to get up, I kept on going dizzy. I could only eat tiny portions of food. When I brushed my hair strands of it fell out, so I showed Matron. Unknown to me, she had called the doctor, who examined me, looking into my eyes and taking blood samples. She said I was jaundiced and anaemic. I had to take tablets and have special dinners; one day liver, the next chicken. My favourite person, as before, was Cook. She made me chicken soup, chicken casserole and chicken pies.

Gradually, after a month or two, I built up my strength. My hair stopped falling out, my eyes weren't jaundiced anymore and I was eating ordinary food. I came out of the sick bay and went back into the girl's dormitory in the annexe.

The woman from the authorities who was at the Naylors that night came to see me. She brought a colleague, so Matron took us all into the staff lounge. They explained that they were there for a reason; to ask me some questions. They started by asking if I liked my new guardian. I told them I missed Miss Wilson, as I had known her from the age of four, and that even though she had been old she had always been very kind to me. As I was talking about her, I had tears in my eyes.

They asked me if I wanted Matron to sit beside me while they questioned me, but I said "No."

"We would like you to tell us from the beginning, when Mr Naylor started to abuse you" said the woman. "Everything you say will be strictly confidential."

This what I told them:

"It all started on a Sunday morning. The Naylors would call me to get into their bed, in between them. There was a lot of laughing, joking and tickling going on, and then Pop started shouting for help. Mrs Naylor got up and went downstairs so I got out of bed too. But Mr Naylor grabbed my nightie, dragged me back and pinned me down on the bed. I started to shout and began kicking but he put his hand over my mouth. He grabbed my hand and put it on his private parts. Mrs Naylor had heard the commotion and shouted 'What's going on up there?' I scuttled back to my room, petrified.

"Every week I went to Brownies and Mrs Naylor would be waiting for me at the top of the unmade road to walk me back home. Then this particular night Mr Naylor came instead. I immediately remembered the last time Mr Naylor met me. He'd given me a piggyback ride, touching my vagina. Seeing him again, I was scared, and I was frightened of the dark. So I knocked on the door of a council house belonging to a lady who always said hello to me. She remarked 'Hasn't anyone come to meet you?' 'No, miss' I said. She picked up a torch and walked me back home, but as we went over the little railway bridge, I heard Mr Naylor rustling in the bushes.

"Next time going to Brownies I deliberately played up, being nasty to the other girls. Brown Owl was flabbergasted at my outburst and drove me home. I was dismissed from Brownies. I missed doing all the activities and going camping. Instead, I was in a load of trouble. However, I was so scared of Mr Naylor. I could not sleep at night, nor could I eat. Because we only had an outside toilet, we had a bucket on the landing to do a pee during the night. I was too frightened to use this bucket in case Mr Naylor was going to abuse me, so I started to wet my bed.

"At school, I was falling asleep in the classroom. I had been chosen to be in a gymnastics show but during practice I could not get up the ropes, I could not jump over the vault and when I was on the balancing beam I fainted, falling and hitting my head. An ambulance took me to hospital but the doctor who examined me said I was OK, I could go home.

"Mr Naylor left me alone for a little while but then it happened. Before going to bed, I had to use the outside toilet, which had no lock on the door. While I was doing a pee Mr Naylor barged into the toilet with his belt in his hand. He was shaking the belt in front of my face, talking in a vulgar, vicious manner, telling me I could shout and struggle as much as I liked because Mrs Naylor was in the bath. No one was going to hear me. He got out his penis. I was still on the toilet and trembling with fear, thinking I was going to die. Then Pop barged in and caught Mr Naylor with his trousers down. Pop went ballistic, shaking his crutches at Mr Naylor and shouting at him, "I knew you was up to no good!" Then Mrs Naylor ran over, going hysterical. She grabbed me and took me upstairs to my bedroom and locked the door."

When I had finished telling them all this I burst into tears, saying, "I don't want to talk about it no more." One of the ladies asked me why I hadn't told anyone.

"Because Mr Naylor said if I told anybody, no one would believe me, he'd tell everyone what a lying little toe-rag I was and that he would have me put away."

The other lady remarked that the Naylors had fostered another girl just like me before I went there, but she had not stayed long either.

Every night I would cry myself to sleep and in my dreams I saw that old man with his baggy trousers, held up with braces, who always wore a shirt with no collar, and with his white moustache tinted yellow nicotine from the pipe he smoked. Pop was my knight in shining armour.

Some nights I would constantly hear Mr Cadman and Matron arguing and hear my name being mentioned. Mr Cadman was so confused. He did not know whether to call me Sheila or Ingrid. He just carried on calling me Williams and other names, bad, names, swearing at me. I was so tired and exhausted. When I saw shadows of the Naylors, I would have to lay my head down to clear my mind.

CHAPTER 3

Life at Hawkridge was more or less the same as it had been before. They had all known me as Sheila and had to get used to calling me Ingrid. Dear, dumpy old Cook still kept calling me Sheila.

And then about a month later Miss Gisborne came to visit me, saying she had found me a place just for girls, in Windsor.

Chapter Four

WINDSOR

Yet again I was sitting in the hallway waiting for my guardian to collect me, this time to take me to Windsor, to a boarding school-cum-orphanage called Lady Mary's. It was not the same leaving as before, all excited and chirpy. It was the opposite.

I had got over my dizzy spells but was very frail and still weak, mentally and physically. I didn't speak to anyone except to say "yes miss, yes sir". I just sat there mesmerised, staring at the clock and listening to the tick, tock. My mind was blank and I was unaware of what was happening around me.

When Miss Gisborne arrived I walked out looking at the ground, without saying goodbye to anyone. As we drove to Windsor the conversation was more or less non-existent. The only thing I did say, shouting in a rage at her, was "I want my own Mother and Father! I know you know because you changed my name! I keep spinning yarns to people about my parents having died in a car crash or in a fire, and I get all confused, telling lies. It gets me into trouble and starts fights." But she just ignored me. We did not stop on the way for tea and cakes as we always did on her visits, nor did we drive through country lanes.

When we reached Windsor I got out of the car and walked, again with my head down, to the front door and only looked up when I heard a lady saying, "Hello Sheila, my name is Jane Burton." I was so surprised when she called me Sheila, because when I had returned to Hawkridge orphanage after living with the Naylors, the people all called me Ingrid. Perhaps there was a psychological reason, to help me get over the trauma of what I had endured?

CHAPTER FOUR

Miss Burton took me by the hand, but I instantly pulled it away, saying "Don't touch me!" Miss Gisborne was disgusted with that and walked away with Miss Burton to the office, with my file. The head girl showed me to a quiet room where I buried my head in a book so that no one would interfere with me. I couldn't read, so I just looked at the pictures. I had no intention of speaking to anyone, knowing I would start to stutter, so I kept my mouth shut.

My guardian left without saying goodbye to me. Miss Burton called me to come and be introduced to the other members of staff: the cook, Miss Darwell and some non-resident staff.

I became Miss Burton's shadow. She showed me the girl's dormitory, which was quite small. She explained that I was the youngest girl, just ten and a half, and that there were head girls and prefects who would be in charge sometimes. The older girls had their own bedrooms and some of them went out to work. It was so different from what I had been used to. The beds were not made; instead the mattresses were folded back in half and the bed linen folded on top.

Miss Burton showed me round the outbuildings: the laundry and scullery-cum-larder room. There were no gardens, only paving slabs and a few swings inside a high perimeter wall. Dawdling behind Miss Burton I could hear people passing by, so I kept on jumping up to see over the wall. Walking round with her was frustrating for me because I was used to either skipping everywhere or, when I was little, running everywhere, and always walked very fast. Miss Burton walked so slowly! She looked very thin and petite, had nimble fingers and thought carefully about everything she did. She explained that every day, before or after school, everyone had to do just one duty, with Miss Darwell giving the orders.

I started to feel hungry. I had missed out on having tea and cakes with Miss Gisborne. The other girls were coming back from school but I could not smell any aroma of dinner drifting through the house.

CHAPTER FOUR

After everyone had changed out of their school uniform, they congregated outside the kitchen. The prefect told me to stand in the row until the cook unlocked the door, then, one by one we picked up a thick piece of bread spread with dripping and a sprinkle of salt on top. My immediate thought was 'I know I've lost a lot of weight, and I'm so hungry!' So I asked the prefect if I could have some more please. She replied, "No, you have to go to church first." I thought it was odd because it was not Sunday yet. However, when everyone had finished eating, they all went to get their hats on. Miss Burton gave me a hat, which I hated wearing. In the past, when I had worn a beret, I would throw it up into a tree and tell Miss or Sir that someone had stolen it at school.

We all then walked across the road to the church. I had my arms folded because I did not want anyone, ie Miss Burton, to hold my hand.

As we walked into the church I was mesmerised by the beauty and tranquillity. In the middle were big chains suspended from the ceiling with a huge cross of Jesus hanging down. There were nuns walking around with lighted candles, and between their breasts they also had chains with big crosses of Jesus. As we walked along you could hear the echoing sound of our feet on the stones.

The service had begun in a small chapel. Everyone knelt down, praying, going round some beads with their fingers. Nothing was spoken in English. All I could think of was when I would get some food, and that my bum was hurting. I had lost so much weight that it felt as though I was sitting on my bones.

I started to get agitated with the hat on my head where I had lost my hair. New hair had started to grow over the bald spot on top and the bristles felt itchy. Then I began to fidget, which did not go down too well with the girls behind me, so they kept poking me in the back. Miss Burton kept whispering to me "Keep still! It's not long now."

By the time the priest was sprinkling holy water at us, I was at boiling point. I got up and threw my hat at the girls behind. Miss Burton escorted me out of the church, where I burst into tears with anger. Sobbing and with a snotty nose I was trying to say "I am sorry Miss, please don't hit me." Miss Burton gave me her handkerchief, took hold of my hand and called me a 'silly billy', saying that no one was going to hit me. I was very relieved.

"Please miss, may I have some dinner?" I said. She was most amused and laughed at me. "Of course you can!" She pinched my cheek then added, "See, you can smile!"

When we got back to the house, the smell of food was most welcoming. After all the duties were done, we stood behind our chairs, waiting to say grace. Everything was so confusing for me. We had just been to church, asking God for forgiveness and to give us our daily bread, and now we were going to ask Him again!

I sat next to Miss Burton and made a pig of myself until my belly was full, conscious though, of the thought that I might be given that diabolical cod liver oil. Instead, Miss gave me some tablets: iron and vitamins.

After dinner, we all retired to the quiet room. The other girls were doing reading, writing or embroidery. I felt jealous of them; they were speaking perfect English and being so ladylike. I was used to climbing trees, tormenting animals and ducking and diving everywhere.

Miss Darwell came into the room and asked me to go with her, and as we left the room the other girls started to laugh at me in a sneaky way. When Miss Darwell was in charge, it was a different kettle of fish. She never smiled or laughed and when she spoke, it was in a dictatorial manner. She said, "I am going to give you elocution lessons". I had to put my arms underneath the table. I was so nervous that my hands were shaking.

In the evening, before going to bed, I spent some time in Miss Burton's sitting room, squatting down on crossed legs to watch her television, with a bag of sweets and her chatting to me. I just nodded my head in response.

That was my first day, and the routine was the same forever afterwards.

This boarding school was for girls only. It was situated in an ordinary road with the church opposite. When I arrived, the school was about to break up for the summer holidays so I didn't go to classes. Each day I had to amuse myself. I had to do extra chores to help Miss Darwell. All the time, she would correct my speech if I said anything wrong. She remarked, "We don't use the word 'chores' here, they are called 'duties'." After doing some 'duties', I went outside, swinging on the swing as high as I could, stretching my neck to say 'Hello!' to the passers-by. I even stood up on the swing to see more, but then I heard 'rat-a-tat-tat' on the window; it was Miss Darwell.

"Get off that swing now!" she shouted. When she wasn't looking, I poked my tongue out and pulled ugly faces at her.

The next afternoon, I went out with Miss Burton for my first day out in Windsor, which is a very picturesque town. Some of the shops were exquisite. I stopped at one glued to the window, watching the people making silk stockings and spinning the cocoon balls into yarns. Other shops that caught my eye were the lace makers and the cobblers, where they were making boots and hand-made saddles, only for the élite. We also went into an arts and crafts shop, where Miss Burton bought an Irish linen tablecloth and asked me to choose the different coloured silk threads. I was more interested in being nosey, though. I went round touching the items for sale, which seemed to agitate the shopkeeper.

Miss Burton then took me to see Windsor Castle. It was spectacular. I stood up on the railings, holding on to the spikes, and poked my head between the metal bars, just staring at it. She kept on calling me to move on. We passed two soldiers with funny hats

CHAPTER FOUR

on, standing in separate boxes. I couldn't stop glaring at them, and again Miss Burton had to pull me away. I asked her if I could go inside the castle, but she replied, "Yes, but not today. One of the prefects will take you at the weekend."

We then stopped at Miss Burton's favourite shop for afternoon tea and cakes. The cups and saucers were very small and dainty and she showed me the ladylike way to pick up the cup with my fingers. Unfortunately, my fingers were too clumsy and I nearly dropped the cup.

As we walked back home I was inquisitive about everything I had seen. I just had to ask her all the ins and outs and whys. I asked her about the soldiers, and why they didn't say 'hello'. She explained to me that they were the Queen's special guards with traditional rules; their uniform, which included the 'Busby' hat, and that they were not allowed to be distracted. I think I wore out Miss Burton with all my questions.

When we arrived back home it was the usual routine: bread and dripping, hat on, church, duty, dinner, elocution lesson, spend time with Miss Burton, then bed.

The weekends were slightly different. A prefect called Susan was in charge of me and I just tagged along behind her. We went inside the castle with the other girls. It was a bit bewildering to me, not understanding the history and with the other girls just fooling around. Another time they took me out, we walked the Long Walk to the Copper Horse, a statue made out of old pennies. I noticed that other, posh, people went by horse and carriage and that there were men on horseback playing something called polo. Again, the other girls were fooling around, smoking cigarettes, frolicking around on the green, flirting with boys and just generally taking the piss out of me.

One day when I had tagged along behind them we all went to the scullery, where one particular girl was making animal figurines. She was talented at making sculptures out of plasticine. She modelled a face

CHAPTER FOUR

and the other girls asked me to guess who it was, but I just shrugged my shoulders. "It's Miss Darwell!" they jeered. Then one of the girls picked up a craft knife, and all the others joined in slicing the nose and ears off, digging and screwing the knife into the eyes, then bashing the face in. I was shocked. I had always put the older girls on a pedestal, thinking how ladylike they seemed, how butter wouldn't melt in their mouths and how 'holier than thou' they were.

On Saturdays after church I didn't have elocution lessons. It was the other girls' parents' night, so I stayed with Miss Burton, watching television. I watched a programme called The Lone Ranger: cowboys and Indians. When the 'bad' bits occurred, I would hide my face with my hands, peeping between my fingers, waiting for the 'bad' bit to finish. At the end of the episode, the Lone Ranger and Tonto, his Indian companion, rode up the mountain, where the two horses reared up and the Lone Ranger shouted, "Hi ho, Silver!". When I saw this, adrenaline pumping through my body with excitement. I waved my hands up high with a gleaming big smile on my face.

"So you like cowboys and Indians?" said Miss Burton.

I replied, "No, Miss, I just like to watch horses."

Then she asked me "Why did you cover your face during the episode?"

"Because I don't like watching good people getting beaten up or killed."

"But you like horses."

"Yes Miss."

I told Miss Burton that when I was staying at the farmhouse, I would go to see the gypsies and scrounge rides on their horses, bartering with them and telling them they could knock on Mrs Naylor's door for bags of rags. She asked, "And did they knock for rags?"

"Yes Miss, but the Naylors had sold the rags to the rag-and-bone man, and a big argument broke out between the Naylors and the

CHAPTER FOUR

gypsies. I never saw them no more." Miss couldn't stop laughing, but I went all silent on her after talking about the Naylors. Miss Burton came and sat next to me, asking if I wanted to talk about what happened when I was sexually abused at the farmhouse.

"No Miss. It's all revealed in the story."

Miss Burton seamed somewhat baffled and asked, "What story is that?"

"My guardian has the story. She told me it's a story about a girl called Sheila and the story's called a file."

She said no more and changed the conversation.

Sundays were a little different. Instead of going to church in the late afternoon, as in the week, we went in the morning. Miss Burton took my hand as we walked across the road and said, "I don't want you to be in any trouble in church today."

When we went in, the church was packed with people. I kept quiet, feeling sad after reminiscing, and knowing that Miss Burton knew what had happened to me.

The service began and everyone had their rosary beads clutched in their hands. The choirboys were singing in Latin: I did not understand what they were singing about, but I knew it was angelic. When it was prayer time, everyone started muttering "Hail Mary", going round the rosary beads with their fingers. Again it was all bewildering, so I just sat in silence. I glanced up and found myself staring at Jesus on that big cross, with nails in his hands and feet, thorns on his head and blood trickling down his face. My heavenly Father. I had had a foster Father on earth who had terrorised me when I was being abused. I had been too frightened to even use the pee bucket on the landing in case I was abused during the night, so I would wet my bed.

All this was going through my mind and I began snivelling, so Miss Burton told me to use a handkerchief. The other girls started poking me in the back again and flicking bits of paper at me. As we all stood up from saying prayers, a girl behind me pulled my hair. I had very long hair and in the past, I had been dragged along the floor by it. Having it pulled now, in church - big mistake!

I turned round, stretched over and started a fight. The church service stopped and we were all led out by Miss Burton.

The whole place was in silence for the rest of the day. When I saw the priest walking through the front door, I knew I was going to be sent back to the orphanage. I buried my face in a book so that no one could see me crying, and tried desperately not to make a noise. The prefect, Susan, came over to me and told me not to worry as the priest often came and went, sometimes staying for dinner.

This was a parents' night and I was wondering whether I would be locked up in a room until the other girls' parents had left, like at the orphanage. I had not seen Miss Burton since church. Miss Darwell took me to the small room and gave me a lecture, not in kind words either. "If there is another outburst like that, next time no mercy will be shown. Now go to Miss Burton and apologise."

When I got to Miss Burton's sitting room, I hesitated, pacing the floor, with all sorts of things going through my mind. I wondered whether or not to by pass the door and just go straight to bed. Then I heard Miss Burton shouting, "How long are you going to be pacing the floor? Just come in!"

I walked in. "I am sorry Miss" I said.

She replied, "You do understand that you have to be punished? There will be no more luxuries."

Then she brought out the tablecloth that she had bought from the art and craft shop. "I am going to teach you how to do embroidery. First, you have to learn how to do the different stitches, practising on this old material. It will teach you to be patient in future."

Every night I sat embroidering and mastering all the different

CHAPTER FOUR

stitches. After that, every time we went to church, weekdays and Sundays, all the other girls sat in front while Miss Burton and I sat behind. No one could pull my hair or flick paper at me any more.

Time flew by so quickly. The school had broken up for the summer holidays and most of the girls went home with their parents. The few of us that were left went on holiday with Miss Burton and other members of staff, to Ventnor in the Isle of Wight. We stayed in a church hall with some girls from other homes.

I had the time of my life. No Miss Darwell, No duties, and I fell in love with the sea and the scenery. We went out every day. We walked to The Needles, went to Cowes to watch the boats, went to the miniature village, all lit up, Went to different festivals, including firework displays and lazed around on the sandy beach. I was in my element. Miss Burton mollycoddled me all the time and I became vaguely aware that she must love me.

Our two-week holiday came to an end. The remaining weeks were spent doing fun things near Windsor - going on picnics, going to the river Thames, swimming in a tributary and watching the Eton boys rowing. But all good things come to an end and it was time for the school term to start. It was to be my first time at Lady Mary's School for Girls, a Catholic Church school for the élite, just across the road.

On my first day of going to school, Miss Burton was fussing over me and making me feel uneasy. She helped me get dressed, doing up my gold and purple tie and making sure my gold and purple sash was neatly round my tunic. She even turned over the tops of my long white socks, which had gold and purple trimming. I was eleven years old and always plaited my own hair, but today Miss Burton picked up the hairbrush and began brushing my hair!

I was gritting my teeth and getting agitated, but every time I put my hands up over my hair she tapped the brush on them to get them down.

"You look beautiful!" she said. She put a handkerchief in my gold and purple blazer pocket and reminded me not to wipe my snotty nose on the sleeve of my white blouse. When she had finally finished titivating, I gave one big sigh of relief.

I walked over the road with the other girls to the school. A nun would always be standing at the main doors and as we passed her, we addressed her: "Good morning, Miss."

In assembly, we were divided up into our classes. My class was small compared with the other school I had been to. My first day went exceptionally well considering I kept my mouth shut all day. The nun walked round the classroom with a ruler in her hand, slapping it into her other hand. This bothered me, so I was unable to concentrate. This was no ordinary school; the teachers were nuns, and they were very strict.

Slowly but surely I began to mingle in with the other pupils. My vocabulary had improved and I was now pronouncing more of my words properly. I was dedicated to the subjects I liked, but English was a 'no go' area for me. In fact, the English nun would often by pass me as if I was a demon and look at me as if I was a waste of space.

On many occasions when Miss Burton took me out, she would stop at a quaint antique shop, just browsing, but one time she went in and bought an antique circular table. I felt deeply proud when she put the tablecloth which I had finished embroidering on this exquisite table. She remarked that I was her ray of sunshine. I became a reformed person. I bounced back to being my bubbly self, tormenting the other girls and getting into mischief. I went round merrily singing while doing my duties, which I did religiously every day.

One day a while later, Miss Darwell stipulated in a scornful manner that I had to peel a bucket of potatoes. I was dumbfounded and angry, knowing that I had done my duty for the day.

"No, Miss!" I said repeatedly. I tried to walk away, but Miss Darwell started to push me. She was pushing me in the back in the direction

CHAPTER FOUR

of the scullery, through the laundry room. I couldn't take any more of her pushing, so I retaliated by pushing her back. She pushed me again and I fell over. Now in a vicious temper, I started kicking out, shouting, "You fucking bitch!"

Miss Darwell picked up a copper stick and started beating my legs with it. I felt it going into my leg like a dagger. When I looked down I was horrified to see blood running down my leg. With all my might, through the anger and pain, I managed to run across the road into the school for help. I ran towards a nun, going hysterical. She put her arms out as if she was going to push me away, so I grabbed the cross she was wearing, and her bunch of keys, and threw them. Then I ripped her habit as I fell to the floor. I think I remember hitting my head on a metal grid when I fell. I do remember a nun passing by me on the floor, and feeling giddy; everyone's' faces looking down at me were just a sea of images going round and round. What happened after that was a blank.

I woke up in the spare bedroom with a bandage on my leg, not remembering what I had done to the nun. There was pandemonium going on, with my guardian, people from the authorities and the priest flitting around. Miss Burton was mollycoddling me, with tears in her eyes. None of us saw Miss Darwell any more. When my guardian told me what I had done, I knew I would be going back to the orphanage. Time had stood still. I was in a world of my own, in silence. When I was surrounded by other people, I could sense a strange atmosphere.

I had tried so hard to be the perfect child, but it wasn't enough. I asked Miss Burton if she was sending me away and she replied in a loving way, "No one is taking you away."

Miss Gisborne explained that I had been expelled from school and that it might be difficult to find another in that area. "The schools have their full quota of pupils" she said. "However there is another option which sounds promising, a special school. First you have to see a psychiatrist."

CHAPTER FOUR

Miss Gisborne came with me to see the psychiatrist but stayed in the waiting room. The psychiatrist asked me a lot of questions, some of them hitting me hard and upsetting me, so that I was unable to answer. This agitated him. Then he asked me to look at some white cards and see if I could visualise some pictures from the top of my head. I looked at them and tried hard to see pictures in a load of scribble. When I told him I couldn't see any pictures, he started to get agitated with me again and my session came to an end.

After my session with the psychiatrist I was constantly on tenterhooks, pacing up and down in silence. I was thinking about people's discrimination against orphan kids because they meant trouble. In the dictionary, it says an orphan is a child without kinfolk. Where does the problem lie? No orphan kid will stand up and tell the nation what really goes on in an orphanage; it's more than their life's worth. The problem stems from the authorities. They make all the 'fuck-ups' and sweep the dirt under the carpet so that everything seems hunky dory.

After a couple of days, still waiting and wondering what was going to happen to me, I saw Miss Gisborne pull up outside. I went to meet her, but when I saw my suitcase in the hallway my stomach turned over. I was mortified and speechless. She tried to comfort me, explaining that the psychiatrist's report had said that I was too intelligent to go to a special school and because I had a speech impediment, it was giving me a mental block.

I begged and pleaded with her not to send me back to Hawkridge, but it was no good.

"It is out of my hands" she said. "The Authorities have said you have to go back to Hawkridge, only for a short time, and owing to the court decision that you are not allowed to live within a ten mile radius of the Naylors."

I didn't care what she was blabbering on about, she was making me angry and I started to shout at her, "I don't want to go back to Hawkridge!"

CHAPTER FOUR

Miss Burton smothered me with cuddles and kisses. Seeing the tears in her eyes, I knew that she truly loved me. But love has no meaning; it was not enough reason for me to stay. I was devastated at having to say goodbye to Miss Burton.

Chapter Five

BACK TO THE ORPHANAGE

As I drove along with Miss Gisborne I was reminiscing about life at the orphanage; remembering the beatings, being called Williams and doing the most undesirable chores. I felt very miserable. I told her that I kept getting a sharp pain in my leg, but she replied, "There's nothing wrong with your leg, Ingrid. You have been on antibiotics."

When she called me Ingrid, I was choked up inside. I could hardly breathe and my head felt as though it was tied up in knots. I jumped out of the moving car and ran away, going frantic in front of the other traffic. A man pulled up his car and helped Miss Gisborne to get me back into her car.

My hands and knees were cut and my coat was dirty. I was sobbing my heart out and trying to get my words out, stuttering that I didn't like her any more and wanted another guardian. I told her that at the orphanage, every time I got a beating, afterwards I was given a bag of sweets. And when my nose was black and blue and swollen, I was given another doll from the attic. She said no more.

When we reached the orphanage, Mr Cadman greeted Miss Gisborne and looked at me with daggers in his eyes. I started to walk away, but Mr Cadman grabbed me by the shoulders. Pushing me back and forth he shouted at me, "You've been in trouble, hitting a nun!"

"I never hit a nun!" I replied.

"So, you never hit the nun?"

"No sir, I pulled her dress and it ripped."

"And I suppose you never jumped out of a moving car neither?"

My guardian just stood there, not saying a dicky bird. I didn't want to see her any more; she knew what had really happened that day.

CHAPTER FIVE

Mrs Cadman took me to the sick bay and bathed my wounds. I mentioned to her the pain in my leg. She looked at it, but said there was nothing wrong. Then I told her that I was going to run away, and she asked me where I would go. "I'm going to be like Dick Whittington and his cat" I said. "I'm going to London to see the Queen and tell her what a fuck-up everyone is making of my life."

Matron could not stop laughing. She told me not to run away just yet because of the pain in my leg. She carried on laughing and taking the piss out of me, thinking I was just seeking attention. She must have told her husband what I had said, because he was watching me like a hawk. Whenever I saw him I felt irritated, not knowing when he would pounce on me or call me bad names.

Within a few days I had settled back into the old routine but the pain in my leg was getting worse. Then one morning I woke up with an agonising pain in my leg. When I looked at it, it was red raw.

I couldn't walk on it, so I was screaming for Miss to come and help me. Everyone arrived on the scene. The staff carried me over to the main house and upstairs to the sick bay to wait for a doctor.

When the doctor came, she gave me injections for the pain and to calm me down, and then examined my leg. She explained to Matron that I had a cork boil; an infection which could have been caused by a tiny fragment of wood still buried in my leg.

I was on tablets round the clock and had to hop everywhere on one leg. Every day I had to sit in my 'boudoir', meaning the hallway, waiting for Matron. When she called me, I went upstairs backwards, on my bum, to the red bathroom. She bathed my leg and applied some ointment.

A few days later as I waited for my treatment, I had another attack of excruciating pain and blood was running down my leg. I went frantic again, shouting for help. I was carried upstairs to the red bathroom and Staff propped me up in the empty bath. Matron pressurised my leg and it was as if a champagne cork of blood and yellow muck exploded into the air. It had released the pressure and some of the pain, but I was left with a hole in my leg, which had to remain open, to heal. I still have a hole and dent scar in that leg today.

While my leg was healing, I spent my days chilling out in the staff lounge. I suppose it was easier for them to keep their beady eyes on me there. I found myself deep in thought, wondering about my parents and what had happened to me when I was a baby. On the spur of the moment, I asked Matron if she knew anything about my mother and father. She paused before answering, and then said, "Are you in an argumentative mood? Because what you are asking me will get you nowhere."

Then I asked her if she would read my story to me.

"What story is that?"

"The one my guardian brings with her, about me when my name was Sheila. It's called the file."

She quickly changed the conversation. I desperately wanted someone to read my story to me. I had asked so many people: my guardian, the Naylors, Auntie and Uncle, Miss Burton, the Hornings, Matron and members of staff, but it always fell on deaf ears, like the three wise monkeys.

My leg was healing, but I was so bloody bored. I was in a bit of a conundrum, being twelve and a half years old. I was too old to play with toys and dolls but too young to go to the quiet room.

I saw Mr Cadman going out to his car, so I decided to ask my favourite member of staff, who's bedroom-cum-sitting room was in the annexe, next to the girls' dormitory, if I could have permission to sit in the quiet room.

"If you go to the quiet room, I don't want any trouble. If Mr Cadman comes home unexpectedly and sees you in there, I never gave you permission, nor did I see you. Do you understand me, Ingrid?"

CHAPTER FIVE

"Yes miss."

So I sneaked into the quiet room, hoping I wouldn't be seen. I snuggled up in the armchair, like a bug in a rug, listening to some fancy music on the wireless. At the same time I was earwigging two new girls' conversation about doing a bunk from the orphanage. They started to disagree about which night to go. The older one of the two, Sandra, said that if they went Saturday night there would not be so much money in the safe, so they decided to go on the Friday night. Their plan was to go over to the main house after lights were dimmed, get into the office, take the key from above the door and steal all the pocket money and church collection money from the safe. I thought this was my best chance to abscond as well. I went out of that quiet room faster than I went in, conjuring up how I was going to persuade the girls to take me with them.

On the Friday night, just before the lights were dimmed, I approached Sandra and Beryl and told them that if they did not take me with them, I was going to tell Miss. I could see the anger on their faces. Sandra said, "You'd better be ready! Go to bed in your clothes."

The lights dimmed and the three of us were up and away, going through the back way of the annexe, over to the main house. The girls had previously left a window in the kitchen open, and we all climbed through. Sandra and Beryl went to the office and I stayed outside to be the lookout. I was nearly shitting my pants, thinking that Mr Cadman was going to appear round the corner. When the girls had got all the money, we climbed back out through the kitchen window, ran past the orchard, up the driveway and away. We hitched a lift to the railway station, but when Sandra and Beryl got the money out to pay the train fare, they realised that it was all sealed in separate transparent bags; halfpennies, threepenny bits, sixpences. They spilled all over the counter and I burst out laughing. I couldn't stop, to the point where I was virtually choking.

CHAPTER FIVE

We eventually got on to the train and the girls told me we were going to Hyde Park. They got their belongings out of their carrier bags. They put bright bleached wigs on, bright red lipstick on and red blusher on their cheeks. They both wore long beads down to their knees. They looked like girls from the glossy magazines. I knew I looked a real hillbilly though. Sandra told me to take off my socks and she threw them out of the train window, so all I had on my feet was sandals.

When we reached Hyde Park station, we had to walk past a lot of shops, which were all lit up with pretty lights, and I suddenly thought - 'What have I done?' We walked through concrete arches into Hyde Park and I was told to sit on a bench. Meanwhile, the two girls were standing on the edge of the kerb, each with a hand on her hip and a fag in the other, They swung their rosary beads, and I knew for sure that this wasn't how rosary beads were supposed to be used.

Two cars pulled up, each with a lone male driver. The girls each got into a car and Beryl shouted at me, "Don't move, we'll be back for you!"

And off they went. Of course, they didn't come back.

I began to get very frightened, and my imagination was running wild. In the end, I was going hysterical, running as fast as I could out of the park. Straight into the arms of a policeman.

I had to go through the formalities, but the police took pity on me. They gave me a cup of hot chocolate and wrapped a blanket round me because I was freezing and all I wanted to do was sleep. The police realised the dilemma I was in, and they knew I would have face the consequences when I got back to the orphanage.

Once I was back there, I first had to answer to Mr Cadman about the other two girls. Then I asked him if I could go to bed. "Yes, you can go to bed, but after you have scrubbed the concrete floor. And don't ask for a kneeler, either. When you are scrubbing, you can think about the money which you stole."

It was the early hours of the morning and I was exhausted

scrubbing that floor. I could only scrub half; my scrawny little body couldn't scrub any more. I fell asleep, right next to the bucket.

In the morning, Matron took me up to the sick bay. Where I had been stretching the muscles in my leg, the hole had gaped open and all this yellow muck was oozing out.

I was in that sick room for nearly three weeks, as I went down with tonsillitis. The worst kind; the streptococcus virus. I was in and out of fevers and it was touch and go whether or not I would have to go to hospital. Matron kept on fussing over me, every day putting violet-coloured ointment on the ulcers at the back of my throat.

"When you ran away to London, did you meet the Queen?" she said.

"No, miss. I just sat on a bench."

When I said that, she rolled up, laughing. On her way out, she said, "You'd better hurry up and get better. You have been chosen to ride on the back of a cowboy horse at Billy Smart's Circus. Yee-ha, Ned!"

She closed the door, laughing.

Matron and the doctor who always looked after me when I was sick nursed me back to health. I do not know whether it was a coincidence or just fate, but the same doctor also nursed me in my adult years. She became a guardian angel to me, and I needed her more than you can imagine.

I made an incredible recovery, and was soon jumping up and down on that bed. I jumped so high you could hear the bed springs creaking. I heard Matron in the background shouting, "You can get up now and get dressed. Go to the quiet room, and don't do any more earwigging! It will get you into trouble."

When I walked into the quiet room, the other kids started on me, saying that I had stolen their pocket money. One of them said Mr Cadman had been ranting and raving, asking them questions all day. Then someone said that the two girls had been found murdered in the park. Miss intervened and said, "That's enough! We know you didn't steal the money, you just went along with the flow." She started laughing again.

Miss Gisborne came to see me, all sweetness and light, dying to tell me about the Christmas outing. But Matron had already let the cat out of the bag.

The big day eventually came and all the kids from the orphanage went by coach to see Billy Smart's Circus. We all had nametags on our backs. When we reached the circus, Miss walked me through the fun fair, round to the back of the arena. My eyes lit up at seeing those magnificent horses, all dressed up for the occasion. The cowboy man asked me if I had ridden on a horse before. I replied, "Yes sir, on the gypsies' horses."

He couldn't stop laughing at me.

Then a short, tubby man in a red coat and tails with long black boots and a top hat arrived. He ruffled my hair.

"You must be Ingrid" he said. "I'm Billy Smart."

The moment came when everyone was mounting their horses. I had a harness round my waist, with a wire suspended from the ceiling. As we rode into the arena, the crowds were cheering and the atmosphere was spectacular. At the end of the show, the horses reared up and I was on top of the world with happiness.

There were only three people I knew who loved horses besides me: Mrs Naylor, Miss Burton and my guardian. Little did I know that Billy Smart was going to crop up again in my life one day.

Over Christmas, I was sent a Christmas present and I had to sit down with Miss to write a thank you letter to the family who had sent it. Miss wrote the letter and I copied it. When she looked at the address where it was going to be sent, she was surprised, and remarked, "This letter is going all the way to Jersey!"

I asked Miss if they were my mum and dad, but she said, "No Ingrid, they are not your parents; just good people." Again, little did

CHAPTER FIVE

I know that in the future I would go to Jersey to meet a family who were also associated with Billy Smart.

Every minute thing that happened to me, I stored in my brain. I thought of what I had done to others, and reflected that God had blessed me with a few days of happiness.

Miss Gisborne came to tell me that it was time for me to move on to a smaller orphanage, in another part of Hertfordshire. She said she knew the people who ran it, who were called Mr and Mrs Horning.

Chapter Six

A LITTLE HAPPINESS

I was not leaving Hawkridge a moment too soon, as I had developed a vicious temper. I would retaliate when anyone hit me, and I had started to resent Mr Cadman calling me 'Williams' and the beatings he gave me. I do remember him being kind; cuddling me up in bed, folding my clothes, giving me a peck on the cheek at night and saving me from the fire, but now, it was a love/hate situation. I was caught between the devil and the deep blue sea with Mr and Mrs Cadman.

Driving along with my guardian to a new place again made me nervous. She saw the worried look on my face and pulled up at a fancy little teashop. When we walked in, everyone knew her and while we were having our tea and cakes, she said that this was where she lived. She reassured me that the Hornings were good people and that she knew them well, but I was still praying, "Please God, make it a nice home."

As we drove through the small village, my guardian pointed out a cinema. "It's right at the bottom of the road where you're going to live" she said.

We drove up an unmade road and she pulled up next to a posh Tudor-style house. The houses opposite were very select too. As we got out of the car, the Hornings came to greet us and shook hands with us. No one had ever shaken my hand before.

Miss Gisborne went to the office with the Hornings, taking my file, my story. By now, that story had been here, there and everywhere. Mr Horning asked a girl who was the same age as me to show me around. She was small and dumpy, with big tits, and introduced

CHAPTER SIX

herself as Pat Doherty. Some other girls were showing off in front of me because I was a new girl.

Pat explained that there were ten boys and eight girls living there. After she had escorted me up and down the stairs, she took me to the girl's dormitory, right at the top of the house. In fact, it was an attic, with a large leaded window. When I looked out, I could see all the grounds and the cinema at the bottom of the road. There were four beds on each side of the room and a small bathroom and spare room at the end. Miss had a private room just outside the dormitory.

Pat showed me my bed, which was opposite to hers. Next to her was a girl called Janet who was strange; she wore big glasses and I noticed yucky spots on her face. She had posters of Elvis Presley and Cliff Richard hanging above her bed and I wondered how I was going to get undressed in front of them.

In the other orphanages I had lived in, we had only listened to wireless speakers, classical and opera music, and at the Naylors, on the farm, it had been the good old Archers. Here, it was a different. Watching telly willy nilly, rock and roll music - this was a whole new ball game for me!

Miss Gisborne left and Mr and Mrs Horning didn't bother me or ask me questions, they just let me mingle in with the other kids. The routine here was similar but more relaxed, and we only had to do one chore. Miss asked the boys if one of them would carry my suitcase up to the dormitory. She was bombarded with volunteers! With the boys, I felt like a princess. The other staff I just knew as Miss or Sir. As at the other orphanages, I never knew their names.

Miss helped me go through my clothes.

"Haven't you got any belongings?" she asked

"No miss" I said.

She took me to the spare room, which was packed with boxes of clothes and shoes and all sorts of things. She explained, "One side of the room are clothes for 'Sunday best' and the other side are playing clothes which you will change into after school. I'll leave you to choose what you want."

I was in that room for ages, scavenging through the boxes with so much excitement, trying on this and that. In the end, I chose a beautiful white angora jumper, a lovely deep blue and green tartan mohair pencil skirt and a pair of low heeled shoes for Sunday best. The play clothes I chose were plain: a skirt and round-neck jumper, but of my own choice.

You should have seen that room! Clothes were scattered everywhere and it took me ages to put it all back, neat and tidy. While I was doing this, I noticed a bracelet on the floor. It looked as if it had silver braiding round each of the blue stones and silver links between the stones.

I knocked on Miss's private door to tell her I had finished and had put everything away. She looked at the things I had chosen and remarked that I had made good choices.

"Did anything else catch your eye?"

"No miss."

"Are you sure?"

I looked down at the floor. "I saw a bracelet, but I never took it miss."

I was always being accused of stealing and Miss saw the worried look on my face. She said, "That bracelet is yours to have, your own possession."

I was stunned, lost for words. But I knew then, and know to this day, that the bracelet on the floor was no coincidence.

Miss handed me my school uniform, which was grey and green with gold trimmings round the edges. We took all the clothes downstairs to be labelled with my name. After that, we both went to the Hornings' private sitting room. The cook brought in a tea tray

CHAPTER SIX

with an assortment of biscuits and I knew this was going to be 'question time' about my past. One of them would start the conversation, being nice, but turning out being nasty, and then I would start to stutter, get angry, and then walk out. I had been down the same road time after time.

But this time it was the opposite, not what I had anticipated. I was asked if I would like to join the Girl Guides on Fridays, join the church choir, which practiced on Wednesday evenings, and go potato picking on Saturdays. I couldn't believe what I was hearing. I was on cloud nine to think how rich I would be with all the money I would earn. I thought, "There is a God after all, answering my prayers."

My dreaded nightmare was still to come, though - school!

I was told I could not wear my bracelet to school, so I had to find a safe place to hide it. That bracelet was precious to me; it was mine. I kept jangling it on my arm and touching the stones. If anyone was going to try to steal it, first they would raid my locker, shake the pillows and look underneath the mattress, so I decided that when no one was looking, I would bury it inside my Sunday best shoes, stuff my socks inside and put them at the back of the wardrobe.

School in the past had been damnation for me; being bullied, being teased about my speech impediment, stuttering and being the school dunce, not able to read or spell. I was always getting into fights and constantly finding myself outside the headmaster's office waiting to be punished with the cane. Then when I got back to the orphanage, I would be punished again for being in trouble at school. If I showed no regret, I would be caned two or three times on my backside. Having the cane so many times, though, made it like water off a duck's back. It was just part of my life.

At Windsor, when my leg had been split open and I had run across the road into the church school screaming out for help, a nun had pushed me away so it became a fight and I was left half-unconscious

CHAPTER SIX

on the floor. A nun who worked for God had always bypassed me in class as if I was a demon. All I had wanted was someone to help me to read and spell. And what did I get? Expelled, for crying out for help. Or was it because I wasn't like the other girls who had good expectations?

Anyway, I knew what to expect, starting yet another school.

The dreaded day came and we all congregated at the front door, waiting for Mr Horning to pass us and give us our dinner money. We walked over a mile, through country lanes, until we reached the school. What I had expected came true: kids calling me bad names and me fighting in the playground. I was dreading going back to the orphanage, thinking that again I would get the cane.

Back at the orphanage I was called into Mr Horning's private sitting room and asked to sit down in the armchair opposite him. He had a bible in his hands and he started to read it to me. He read the verses about how people mocked Jesus, and Jesus said, "If people provoke you, turn the other cheek." Mr Horning reading the bible to me was my punishment and I felt guilty and sad. That hurt me more than a caning.

The next day I ignored the kids pushing, shoving, and calling me bad names. I was on my own in the playground, as though I had been sent to Coventry. During my English lesson, the teacher explained to me that all the children in school were divided into groups: Red, Blue, Green or Yellow. She told me I was in Blue and gave me a blue badge. In the background, I could hear some other kids sighing. Just before the bell went for playtime, the teacher asked me to go with him to the staff quarters. He explained that he wanted me to leave the class early in the morning and in the afternoon, to prepare tea and snacks for the staff, then stay to clean up afterwards. I knew the reason why: they must have seen how unhappy I was in the playground.

In my first PE class I was nervous about having to wear a short pleated skirt. I was conscious of the dent in my leg caused by being beaten with that copper stick. It was noticeable to everyone, because I kept pulling my skirt down while we were playing netball. My PE teacher began to get annoyed with me, but realised what was wrong. She took me back to the changing rooms and gave me a pep talk about my leg. She chose a plaster, a similar colour to my skin, and slapped it on. "Now, get out there and play!" she said.

I went out and ran like the wind, bouncing that ball. No one could catch me. I was the best and no one could believe how I played so well; everyone was mesmerised. My PE teacher, Mrs Crockett, was surprised. Harpenden School was know for its excellence in sport. There were silver cups in glass cabinets everywhere! I became a star, the school hero. No one bullied me or called me bad names any more, and Mrs Crockett became another guardian angel.

My life had been transformed, and I was happy and contented. I was happy going to Guides, earning all my badges. Choir practice was difficult for me, not being able to read very well, but Mr and Mrs Horning helped, playing their piano while I rehearsed the hymns and memorised the words. It was sensational being able to sing out loud, not stuttering once.

Potato picking was hilarious. We had to wait at the bottom of the road for the tractor to pick us up, and then we all stood in the trailer. Driving through the village, we would shout and wave at the local people like a bunch of hooligans.

The farmer took us to the fields he wanted us to pick, then drove in front of us, dropping sacks for us to fill. When he wasn't looking, we had potato fights. We would be picking all morning, and after collecting our hard-earned money we congregated in the local coffee shop to play the jukebox and do the hand jive. If Saturday potato picking coincided with away matches of hockey or netball, I had to forfeit the potato picking and my one pound.

CHAPTER SIX

In a sense Mrs Crockett adopted me. She would pick me up from the orphanage and drive me in her car to the pick-up point for the coach. We played all over Hertfordshire County, winning cups. After playing away matches, I would go back with Mrs Crockett and stay at her house until the next day. Any time I was in trouble and had the bible read to me, Mrs Crockett would come to the orphanage and bail me out.

Instead of the one pound I had to forfeit, I did some cleaning for the little old lady who lived in a bungalow opposite the orphanage. I did this twice a week in the evenings, and as well as getting my one pound, there was an added bonus of sweets, cakes and scrumptious chocolate honeycomb fingers.

During the winter months, the Hornings divided some of the garden into plots for a competition. Everyone had to enter, but only eight would be chosen to have a plot, and I was one of the eight. Unknown to us, Mr Horning had asked an outsider from the village to come every now and then to inspect the plots. Each week I religiously attended to mine: weeding, planting vegetables and flowers, all out of my own money. Some of the other kids just lazed around and their plots looked neglected.

In the end, I won the prize. I think Mr Horning had thought one of the boys would win, because the prize was a trip to Portsmouth. With Mr Horning and Miss, I had a day trip on a boat called the Crested Eagle and a look round the Daffodil ship. I had lots of pampering from the sailors and other crew.

Miss Gisborne did not come to see me much during this time, because I was always out doing activities. At this orphanage though, there was a telephone in the corridor for everyone to use, so she often phoned to check that I was all right. One particular week when she phoned, I told her that the vicar at the church had asked me if I would like to be confirmed along with the other children. She explained that

CHAPTER SIX

she would have to discuss the matter with the Authorities. It was not the answer I wanted to hear, but I wasn't upset either.

I had been praying to God for years in all different churches: Catholic, Baptist, Methodist and Church of England. I had been baptised in the name of Sheila, when I was little. The church I belonged to now was different; I was in the choir and got paid half a crown every week, and five shillings for weddings.

Miss Gisborne came to the orphanage one day. I had not seen her for months. She was pleased to see me and I was pleased to see her, but I was a bit on edge, wondering what she had to say. We all went into Mr and Mrs Horning's sitting room, and after discussing how well I had done with my reading and other schoolwork, Miss Gisborne explained that she had permission for me to be confirmed.

"But first, you have to get baptised in the name of Ingrid" she said.

"Why was I called Sheila?" I asked.

"It is only known by the powers that be; the GOV-ER-MENT."

Miss Gisborne had an irritating habit. At the end of her visit, she would always tell me something which she felt a bit apprehensive about telling me. I always knew though, by the expression on her face. This time it was: "I'm sorry, but I have to tell you that you have another name; a middle name, Emilia."

I looked straight at her and paused, stunned. I was thinking that my guardian was the one with the mental block, knowing about my name! She was the one who had told me, three years before, that my proper name was Ingrid, so she was the one needing a psychiatrist! I asked her if I could have my birth certificate, but she replied, "I'm sorry but I have not got all the answers to all your questions."

Then she started to walk out, but I started to shout at her, "Give me my fucking birth certificate!"

The Hornings led me out of their sitting room, but I was in a rage by this time, still shouting at Miss Gisborne "Go on, fuck off to your car, piss off!"

CHAPTER SIX

I ran outside to the garden, sobbing my heart out and wondering about the family I never had.

The Hornings left me alone in the garden, even when it was getting dark. Then I heard someone walking towards me, and when I turned round, it was my PE teacher. She had bought me a small gold cross on a chain to wear at my confirmation.

I was baptised and confirmed in my real name, dressed all in white, and took my first Holy Communion. When the priest put his hands on my head to bless me, I burst into tears. Mrs Horning had to sit with me at the altar, to comfort me. I was emotionally upset. I loved my heavenly Father, and Pop, and Miss Burton; those who had been truly good to me when the chips were down.

As time went on, my life came to another turning point. At school, during assembly, it was announced that Mrs Crockett, my PE teacher, was leaving to have a baby. I couldn't believe what I was hearing. I was devastated, gutted! My whole outlook changed; I became bad-tempered and argumentative. I developed an attitude of not caring. I had no motivation, at school or at the orphanage.

The nights started to get dark early and the winter began to get dismal. The orphan kids had to leave school early and were not allowed to do detention, because of having to walk through country lanes in the dark.

Christmas was not far away, but at choir practice, rehearsing the carols, I was getting all my words muddled up. At school, we had already started to make our Christmas cakes. The cookery teacher never liked me; she thought I was a waste of space. Cookery was not my forte. Everything I cooked was a disaster. My Christmas cake was hollow in the middle, which took a whole pot of jam to fill, and the marzipan kept sliding off the sides. Everyone in the class kept laughing, taking the mickey, but the teacher was not amused. My cake was pathetic, but I didn't even care.

CHAPTER SIX

Every afternoon I had to do detention, forfeiting all the other classes, including sports. The cookery teacher made me stir all the icing, adding drops from the 'blue' bag every day. It was so tedious. When she didn't have her beady eyes on me, I just sat there, staring at the other Christmas cakes that were perfect, and thinking to myself how I could destroy them.

I only pretended to look interested when my teacher began to ice the cakes. She filled an icing bag up and told me to do some decorating on the icing board. It was amazing! I was gifted at this; it came naturally to me. When the teacher gave me the job of decorating the other kids' cakes, it gave me great pleasure. I did piping, trelliswork, flooding in and scrolls. It helped me tremendously to bounce back to being happy, after the loss of my PE teacher.

In sewing class, I made a white crimplene baby dress. I made it all by hand and embroidered the yoke. I made that dress with love and admiration for the person who had taken me under her wing and been kind to me, got me out of trouble, and most of all, believed in me.

We had our carol service in St Albans Cathedral. The choir was in the gallery and I sang some of the verses on my own. On Christmas Day and Boxing Day, I stayed with Mr and Mrs Crockett and her bump.

After Christmas, Miss Gisborne came to see me, again with the file under her arm. This time she told me it was time for me to move on. I was to go to live with a family called the Culvers, who lived in Hemel Hempstead, and she wanted me to get settled before starting work. There are no words to describe how I felt, having to go and live with a family again. All the abuse I had endured before was soul destroying.

At school, in assembly again, the Headmaster announced that I was leaving, even though I was not yet 15 and the other kids in my class would still have two more terms until the end of the year. He

CHAPTER SIX

asked me to step up on to the stage. All the teachers were there and they presented me with the biggest box of chocolates I had ever seen. It was with their sincere gratitude for making their tea and snacks over the past years.

I was then handed a small silver cup with my name inscribed on it, for all-round sports achievement. The headmaster presented me with two certificates for apprenticeships: sewing and machining clothes and cake decorating. Then he presented me with a book called The Science Book of Hairdressing. That was my goal in life, then.

I was devastated to have to leave that school and the orphanage where I had been the most happy.

Chapter Seven

THE CULVERS

It was heartbreaking saying goodbye to Mr and Mrs Horning and all the staff who had continually helped me through my highs and lows. As we drove away, I was in floods of tears. My guardian was keeping a low profile, and I just kept my lips sealed. There was an atmosphere between us. She was huffing and puffing, then she stopped the car.

"We can't go on to the Culvers with this atmosphere" she said.

I was fourteen and a half and I suppose I had my own values. Growing up with deceptions and half-truths being told, I had become paranoid and was disbelieving everyone around me. This was my downfall, as it made me feel insecure all the time.

"I don't make all the decisions" said Miss Gisborne.

"No, it's only the Powers That Be!" I said sarcastically. "Were they afraid I was getting too clingy with my PE teacher and spilling the beans about the abuse and having to live with a pervert at the age of ten?"

She sighed, and I could see tears in her eyes.

"I've been making enquiries about getting you a hairdressing apprenticeship. I promise you that in the meantime I will get you a part-time job so that you will have your own space away from the family. If you're still unhappy or things don't work out, you have my telephone number. Can we call it a truce now?"

I gave her a half-hearted smile and we carried on driving.

Meeting the Culvers was not as I had imagined. Mr Culver was tall and thin with a bald head and a charming smile. Mrs Culver, in contrast, was extra large, with layers of blubber showing from tits to toes and sweat marks underneath her arms. The first thought that went through my head was 'God only knows how she manages to sit on the toilet!'

The two girls were twins, much younger than I was. The way they spoke to me, they sounded like two spoilt brats. My guardian saw the expression on my face and before she left she whispered in my ear./

"Please try and make a go of it" she said.

Mrs Culver brought out a big bowl of crisps as a get-together before tea. The children stood on their chairs and stretched across the table, throwing crisps at each other, then scoffed the lot. No 'please', 'thank you', or saying 'excuse me'. I was dumbfounded.

The Culvers were trying to make conversation with me and suggesting that I might like to call them Auntie and Uncle. Big mistake! I had been down that road in the past. I shocked myself by my reply.

"I've never called anyone mum or dad or auntie or uncle" I said. "Mr and Mrs Culver will be fine."

Welcome to my life with the Culvers. It was going to be short lived.

During the week I was Mrs Culver's skivvy, doing all the housework and going to and fro with her shopping list to the corner shop. She didn't pay for her groceries; they were always 'on tick'. I was tempted to ask for an item for myself, but I never did, as I was so used to having my own money.

That same week, I was surprised to see Miss Gisborne back. I wondered if the Culvers had complained about me being rude. But it was because she had found me a part-time job in a coffee house-cum-restaurant and she wanted to take me herself to the interview.

When I overheard her telling all this to Mrs Culver I was rubbing my hands together, thinking 'Thank you, God, thank you!"

Mrs Culver did not seem too happy and was raising her eyebrows. I couldn't wait to get into my guardian's car.

CHAPTER SEVEN

I distinctly remember my interview being on a Friday. The owners were Miguel and Roseanna, but everyone called her Rosie for short. They showed me around and explained what the job entailed: laying and clearing the tables, washing up and making coffee from the machine behind the counter. Miss Gisborne was happy for me, and I was too. She gave me the money for my bus fares and extra money for myself. I started work the very next day, Saturday.

The coffee shop was packed solid with young people, laughing, joking and fooling around. It reminded me of the coffee shop in Harpenden, but all that happiness I knew had now gone. That first day I was very nervous and I did panic, but Rosie nurtured me through. It was hard work trying to keep up with the customers; there was no time for skiving! But when we had a quiet period, all the staff sat down for a meal.

Earning my own money gave me joy and satisfaction, but being under age, I could only work certain permitted hours: Saturdays and Sundays all day, then during the week, in the evenings from four until seven. Miguel sneaked me some extra hours as a goodwill gesture. After work, I dreaded going back to the Culvers because as soon as I got back, I was asked to hand over my wages. I was angry. No way was I going to give her my hard-earned money! When Mr Culver came home I had to answer to him, but he was a quiet man and did not really care what went on. He just went along with the flow.

One evening an ice-cream van pulled up and Mrs Culver bought everyone an ice cream, barring me. Yes, I was hurt! I had tears in my eyes, but it wasn't the last or only time. When friends came to stay overnight, I had to sleep on the floor, and when her sister came to stay, I was permanently sleeping on the floor in the corridor.

In the orphanage, you never dared tell tales on other members of staff. Who was going to believe an orphan kid? You just had to keep your mouth shut and store it all in your mind. However, I was wiser

CHAPTER SEVEN

and bolder now, so I phoned Miss Gisborne to tell her all the shenanigans that were going on. Meanwhile I just kept a low profile. For Mrs Culver it was 'Do what I say, not what I do', meaning, carry on with the housework when you're not at that coffee shop. I paid no heed to anything she said and went down to the coffee shop.

Miguel asked me to put posters up in the coffee area. They were for a dancing competition, with Joe Brown and his band, and the entrance fee was five pounds. Rosie remarked, "You should go. Have some fun!"

She was dancing the twist in front of me, with me laughing my head off, when Miss Gisborne walked in. I had to explain quickly that I was not working, just putting up some posters, and showed them to her.

Miguel took us both round to the back of the coffee shop to speak in privacy. Miss Gisborne asked me to listen, and not interrupt her.

"I've been speaking to the Culvers and they have explained to me that when she asked for your wages, it was to keep them safe, but you went into a frenzy and didn't give her time to explain" she said. "With the ice cream business, she did not think you deserved one, owing to you throwing the money at her. The sleeping situation, she says, was an emergency. The money which I give you is not out of my own pocket. You are under Government care until you are eighteen, and are provided an allowance for your keep, clothing, and eight pence a week pocket money. While you were earning your own money, your pocket money was being banked, over the years, by the Hornings and it belongs to you."

"Is the Government paying the Culvers just to put a roof over my head?" I said. "For someone who just doesn't exist? I tried to join in with their conversations but found myself starting to stutter and was cut out of them. Is the Government paying for me to sleep on the floor? Mrs Culver never says 'thank you' for doing the housework,

CHAPTER SEVEN

never says how nice the house looks, and when I get dressed up, no one says how nice I look. I do all the errands to and from the shop and the only one who ever praises me is the shopkeeper."

I was feeling deeply hurt and kept on apologising to Miss Gisborne. I felt guilty for making her a referee. I knew it would be payback time regarding the Culvers. I should have kept my mouth shut. In the end, I was in floods of tears. I knew that the conversation between my guardian and myself would be written in my file: an obnoxious teenager.

As my guardian was leaving, she asked if I would like to go boogieing. "Yes please!" I said.

"I'll tell the Culvers that you are going to a ball, and we'll go out shopping" she replied.

I was happy as a sandboy. I was in the mood for dancing now. At the coffee shop, when the wireless or jukebox were on, I started to tap my feet and wiggle my hips. When I was doing Mrs Culver's cleaning I pretended the broom was my dancing partner, doing the jive. Scrubbing the toilet, I wiggled my bum. I imagined singing with a tin of polish as a microphone, until Mrs Culver switched off the wireless. That woman just did not like me being happy for some reason.

Miss Gisborne and I went shopping. We walked for hours round all the boutiques and fashion shops. In the end I chose a white silk blouse with puffed sleeves, a four-inch black belt, a red flared skirt, a white petticoat with layers of net and frills, a black angora bolero and a pair of white high-heeled shoes. I felt as though I would be the belle of the ball.

When we had finished doing all our shopping, we went back to the coffee shop where I worked. I showed everyone my new outfit. Rosie kept on urging me to try it on, so I did. When I appeared back into the coffee room after changing, everyone was startled. Miguel gave me a wolf whistle and they were all very happy for me. They said I looked very trendy!

CHAPTER SEVEN

The Culvers drove me to the dancing competition, which was held in a hotel function room on the outskirts of Hemel Hempstead. Driving along in that huge black car was a nightmare, with their two children touching my new outfit with their sticky mitts, pulling at my bracelet and kicking my feet. The thoughts going through my head were not charitable.

When we arrived there were crowds of people congregating outside. Mrs Culver escorted me into the hotel, being very charming to everyone. Before leaving, she told me, "No smoking, no drinking alcohol, no hanging around outside with boys!"

I thought she would never go. When she did, I gave one big sigh of relief.

As I walked into the function room I was mesmerised by the lights. Most were illuminating the stage, which looked magnificent. When Joe Brown appeared on stage, everyone clapped, whistled and cheered. At first I felt like a little girl, lost among the crowds, but then I met some friends I knew, from Harpenden.

The first dance was the twist, and I was in my element. The second dance was the jive and I was not short of partners. I just danced the night away and could not care less about my troubles or my gremlins. I could have carried on dancing until the next day.

Then the winners were announced.

"First prize for the twist goes to… INGRID! The first prize for the jive goes to… INGRID and her partner!"

There were other prizes for other dances, like the jitterbug and the bugaboo. We all had to step up on to the stage to receive our prizes. I was nervous and excited both at the same time. Joe Brown gave me a kiss on the cheek and I shook hands with the band. It was awesome! I did not make a speech; I was too frightened that I would look a booby if I started to stutter.

The Culvers picked me up on the dot. They confiscated my prize

CHAPTER SEVEN

of a box of fifty Weights cigarettes and a big box of chocolates. I'm sure the prizes had been mixed up, but I didn't care, even though I didn't smoke. I only had a few chocolates - the Culvers scoffed the rest. But it was not just about winning a prize, it was the fantastic feeling that I had won.

I had made a friend, Brenda, who lived on the same estate as me, so we decided to meet up the next day and go down town. I had never had a friend while I was living at the Culvers, only workmates who were much older and more mature than I was.

I got dressed just in plain clothes, nothing fancy, and asked Mrs Culver very, very nicely if I could have permission to go out. She looked at me and wanted to know the ins and outs, and who I was meeting. I knew by her voice that she was being cocky and sarcastic, that this was going to be payback time for Mrs Culver. I explained in a calm, collected way that the friend I had made lived on our estate and that her name was Brenda. Mrs Culver said, "Are you talking about Brenda with the bleached white hair, the one who's always in fancy clothes?"

"Yes. Why?"

"Because she is the biggest tart on the estate and you are not going out with her. Anyway, the housework hasn't been done."

I had not been rude or obnoxious in making my request, so now I just stood there, dumbfounded. I could feel my heart pounding. No way was I going to beg, so like a bull in a china shop, I ran to the front door, but she had locked it. Then I saw red. I went for her.

Both of us were like alley cats, pushing, shoving, and pulling each other's hair. Trying to get away from her was virtually impossible because she was so fat. She barged in front of me, no matter which way I went. In the end, I jumped out of a window and was away as fast as I could run. I could hear Mrs Culver shouting in the background, "Come back, and come back now!"

CHAPTER SEVEN

Go back for what? To do all the chores and the errands with no please or thank you? Like Little Jack Horner who sat in the corner, because I could not help myself from stuttering.

The police picked me up and I was taken down to the police station, in shock after what had happened.

Miss Gisborne collected me from there and took me back to her place. The police had to make out a report and she had to report to the Authorities.

The 'powers that be' decided that I had to go back to Hawkridge. I lost out more than you can imagine. And for what? Mrs Culver's payback time. I knew in my heart I was jumping out of the frying pan into the fire, going back to Hawkridge and Mr Cadman.

Chapter Eight

HAWKRIDGE AGAIN

I did not relish the thought of going back to the orphanage, but I had no choice. It was a Jekyll-and-Hyde life at the Culvers. At the coffee shop my spirits were high, while being with the Culvers was the opposite, damnation. It was noticeable for everyone to see, including my guardian.

When we reached the orphanage, Matron was there to greet us. She could not believe how much I had grown. I was now nearly fifteen and she found that I had grown into a beautiful young woman. I was not the snotty-nosed kid getting up to mischief anymore. I still had a child-like attitude though, laughing at the least little thing, and I still had the high spirits. Mr Cadman just stood and stared at me as if I was a ghost.

We all went into the staff sitting room to discuss my future. My guardian had been a busy little bee over the past weeks: She had already arranged for me to have an apprenticeship in hairdressing, and she had also arranged for me to attend the interview to start work. Her plan was that eventually I would have a flat share.

While everybody was chatting away, I noticed the solid silver horse and carriage I had had on my birthday cake when I was seven years old. Matron remarked "Yes, it is yours when you are ready to leave."

I left them all there, said my goodbyes to Miss Gisborne and walked with my suitcase over to the annexe with Miss. She gave me my own bedroom, an alcove off the landing. I had my own dressing table and a single wardrobe. The only disadvantage was that everyone had to walk through where I was sleeping to get to the dormitories.

CHAPTER EIGHT

While Miss was sorting out which clothes I might need, she was interrupted by the phone ringing. When she returned she said "It was Mr Cadman on the phone, asking for you to go to his office. Don't worry, you're not getting a caning, it's most probably just for a general chat."

As I walked over to the main house I was feeling apprehensive and could feel my heart racing. By the time I knocked on his door and Mr Cadman said "Enter!" I was a bag of nerves.

I stood there, waiting for him to swivel round in his chair. When he did, he just glared at me, and then he took hold of my hands and started to swing them from side to side. Then he told me to do a twirl.

"What a beautiful person you have turned into!" he said.

I was unnerved by this, and the way he was looking at me was putting the fear of God into me. But I might have been just over-reacting.

My big day finally came, and even though I was nearly fifteen I still had to comply with the rules and sit in the hallway, waiting for my guardian to take me to my interview. Before going, Matron kept on titivating my hair and wishing me luck. I needed all the luck in the world. I felt I looked like a hillbilly!

Miss Gisborne drove us to Mrs Hoffman's Salon in Apsley. We had a long discussion about what was expected of me on starting the apprenticeship, and my wages, which were extremely low. Miss Gisborne kindly explained to the proprietor that I was dyslexic, and asked if it would cause a problem.

I did not know what to say, I was so embarrassed. I felt as though I was a nobody, an imbecile, because I couldn't spell. Mrs Hoffman called over the other experienced hairdresser, Brenda, who was going to be my mentor, and explained to her that I was dyslexic and asked her if it would be a problem at the college of hairdressing. Brenda replied that it wouldn't, because the exams were done in multiple choice format.

CHAPTER EIGHT

I tagged along with Brenda, through to the back room. She showed me where all the potions and lotions were kept, then we had a chat. She told me that the shop next door was a bakery which made freshly-baked cream doughnuts, apple doughnuts and jam doughnuts, and every day the baker handed over the fence a bag of assorted doughnuts. She went on to say that she herself lived near Hawkridge, next to the arches, so we could catch the same bus to and from work. She said that from Thursday to Saturday the shop was chock-a-block with clients, most of them from the paper mill factory further down the road.

"Be very careful what you say to the clients" she warned. "They are very nosey and will want to know all your business. Just be polite, and if anyone is sitting in the waiting area, you'll have to make them tea or coffee. We all decided not to discuss or mention that you live in an orphanage, but don't be concerned, because you will be with me all day.

"On Monday nights, I'll be taking you to the college at Finsbury Park and on Wednesday nights, after work, we all go to the bowling alley with the hairdresser's team. Have you ever played bowls before?"

I hadn't. She said it was good fun and we would all have a bite to eat in the café opposite the bowling alley to end the night.

By this time my guardian had finished discussing the financial side of things with Mrs Hoffman, who was the spitting image of the singer Nana Mouskouri. Brenda was a blonde bombshell and I was just simple old me.

I had time on my side to change my appearance, but not yet, not just yet. I had a few gremlins in my mind, such as the way I jumbled my words up when I got nervous, then started to stutter. I knew I would have to use all my energy and resources to accomplish my ambition.

The one thing I had always wanted out of life was a home of my

CHAPTER EIGHT

own. Now I had the chance to have a flat share, I would have to put all my gremlins to one side and concentrate, to work hard and save my money.

Miss Gisborne and I left with a good result; I had been accepted for the apprenticeship. On the way back to the orphanage, she stopped at the tea shop to give me one of her pep talks. She explained about the money situation and said the government would pay for my college fees, my equipment and my uniform.

"Out of your wages you can pay for your night out at the bowling alley" she said. "At the moment, you can only work twenty hours, because you have a couple of months to go before you're fifteen. So it would benefit everybody if you work from Thursday to Saturday as it's their busiest time. Plus, you'll earn extra money, from the customers tips."

I felt in my element, and when we got back to the orphanage I had a big grin on my face. Everyone else was happy for me too.

In my spare time, I was expected to do some chores. As Mr Cadman said, "You can work to maintain your keep now, girly, and as one of the cleaners is off sick, you can polish the dining room."

"Yes sir."

Miss and Sir helped me to move all the tables and chairs to one side of the room. They gave me a big tin of polish, which had a stick in it. Miss explained that you put a little bit of polish on to the stick and sprinkled it evenly across the floor. Sir brought in the buffer machine and showed me the on/off button and how to work it, and then they both left.

I had never done this before, but I was in a happy mood and felt like dancing. I got hold of the stick and threw a big dollop of polish on the floor, and another dollop here, another dollop there, until there was a dollop everywhere. But when I turned on the buffer machine, it was like a little robot and I just could not control it. It was churning up all the polish and splattering it all over the walls. I had put too much polish on the floor and the buffer was sliding in all directions.

I started to scream out for help, and when Miss came in she couldn't stop laughing. Then Sir walked in, and immediately pulled out the plug. However, when Mr Cadman arrived, he went berserk. He asked me what the fuck I was doing and started pushing me and clouting me round the head. He told me to get out of his sight and said I was a fucking imbecile. He carried on shouting at the staff, saying, "God help the poor bastards at the hairdressers, they'll all come out of there scalped!"

I kept my distance from Mr Cadman and helped Cook in the kitchen as much as I could. Every time Cook looked at me, she could not stop laughing. She said, "Mr Cadman did not mean what he said, he was just annoyed. He had to get outside cleaners in because the buffer was clogged up with polish."

The gardener came into the kitchen for his usual afternoon tea and cakes and made a joke. "Don't worry, you will be getting your own flat soon and you can polish to your heart's content!" he said, laughing.

The rest of the week I did errands for Matron, and in the evenings I took her dog out for a walk. The dog was a miniature poodle called Precious, and it was a vicious little thing, but it was Matron's pride and joy.

Thursday finally came, thank God, and I was up and had my breakfast in the kitchen. Matron gave me some money for my bus fare and a snack, and gave me the hairdresser's card to show the ticket collector on the bus. She told me that the bus stopped right outside the hairdresser's shop.

The rest of the week went extremely well. The hairdresser's was packed, but Brenda nurtured me each day. I was like a blue-arsed fly, sweeping the floors, cleaning the mirrors with methylated spirit,

CHAPTER EIGHT

washing out the towels, preparing the customers with gowns and mackintoshes and making tea and coffee all day.

The baker shouted over the fence, handed me a bag of doughnuts, and asked me if I was the new girl. I just nodded my head, as I was more interested in having a doughnut than a conversation.

After weeks and months passed, I had my fifteenth birthday and now I was in a full time apprenticeship. I became more experienced and I was exceptionally nice to all the customers. I gave them an excellent hair wash and head massage and earned generous tips. I got on with Brenda like a house on fire. We went bowling every week, and she took me to the hairdressing college in London. Our tutor was none other than Raymond 'Mr Teasy Weasy', and I was chosen to be his model for the night.

I had the most beautiful hair and when he asked me for permission to cut it all off, I was a bit apprehensive. While he was cutting my hair, he was explaining everything he did to the other hairdressers and just swept all my hair to one side with a flick. When he finished, my appearance had been transformed. Then I had a makeover by a beauty consultant from Harrods. I was over the moon with excitement; I was the star for that night, and it made me feel good about myself.

When I got back to the orphanage, everyone was staring at me. Matron said that I looked like a film star and Miss said I looked fantastic. Mr Cadman just stood there, looking at me in utter disbelief.

The next day when I caught the bus, even the conductor had to look twice, and when I walked into the shop, Mrs Hoffman was thrilled that the famous Mr Teasy Weasy had done my hair. It was the gossip among the clients.

Brenda knew that I was earning a pittance and had to rely on tips for extra money. She and Mrs Hoffman sorted out their make-up and gave me some.

CHAPTER EIGHT

On Sundays, Mrs Hoffman would take me out with her family to their boat on the Norfolk Broads, and during the week she would give me a lift back to the orphanage to save on bus fares. She almost adopted me. But the only person I told my inner thoughts to was Brenda. I told her in confidence that when I got my flat share I was going to get my birth certificate and my file and try to find my real mother and father.

After work in the evenings, I carried on walking Matron's dog. One particular night, I tripped and fell and the dog ran loose. I was in a terrible state, knowing that the dog was Matron's pride and joy.

As I fell, my stockings were torn and my legs were bleeding. A man helped me up and caught the dog but I felt so embarrassed when he took it upon himself to walk me home. He made conversation, asked me my name and told me his name was Nigel. When we got to the orphanage, I walked straight past the entrance and carried on walking to the next house down the lane. Then I said "Thank you, and goodbye."

The next evening when I got back to the orphanage, lo and behold, Nigel was at there. He had brought red roses and a box of chocolates for Matron and a box of cigars for Mr Cadman. Then he asked the Cadmans if he could have their authorisation to take me out.

I could not believe what I was hearing. I felt so stupid, knowing that all I wanted to do was to ditch him in case someone saw me walking Matron's dog with a strange man. I didn't want to get into any trouble and it might put the mockers on my plans for a new flat.

The next day at work, I told Mrs Hoffman and Brenda what had happened and both of them were in stitches and thought it was hilarious. During the day, both of them kept having outbursts of laughing.

Nigel and I went out on dates. We went to the pictures, went on picnics, spent time in the coffee shop, and he came bowling with us.

CHAPTER EIGHT

The only thing I did not like was when he kissed me goodnight. I could feel his goofy front teeth on my mouth, which made me cringe, and each time he kissed me I would wipe my mouth. In all, though, he was a gentleman and his vocabulary was excellent. He was also a very generous man and I could have anything I desired.

Then the day came when he was going to introduce me to his parents. I was on tenterhooks all day as I did not have much of a choice where clothes were concerned, and the money I had stashed away was for my flat. Brenda had to rescue me. She brought in some clothes for me to wear - it was lucky that we were the same size. She gave me a nice black, sloppy, roll-neck jumper, a light blue miniskirt, black tights and black buckle shoes.

The next day was the big day. Nigel was going to meet me straight after work, picking me up in his father's car to go for a nice evening meal. Brenda washed and set my hair, Mrs Hoffman put on my makeup and for the final touches, Brenda sprayed all different coloured lacquer on my hair. She said that I was all dressed up like a glamorous model.

I was very excited, but at the same time, I was very nervous. Brenda took me into the back room and said, "Here, have a couple of puffs of my cigarette." I had never smoked before; this was my first time and I started to choke. I did not know what she had given me, but my face went bright red and all I could do was keep giggling. I felt I didn't care about anything. I was away with the fairies, with my rainbow hair!

But when Nigel picked me up he seemed ashamed of my appearance. He made a string of excuses for not introducing me to his parents; they must have been very superior. He dropped me back at the orphanage and didn't give me a goodbye kiss. I didn't care about that, because it meant I wouldn't have to feel his fangs on my mouth anymore.

CHAPTER EIGHT

Walking through the orphanage, I tried not to look conspicuous and was sheepishly walking along the hallway when all of a sudden, Mr Cadman shouted out. "Hoy, come back here, girlie!"

My heart was in my mouth and I tried very hard not to laugh, but as I turned round, I saw the staff and the other kids in the background sniggering. When Mr Cadman looked at me, he went bonkers. He started pushing and shoving me, asking what I had done, and told me to get the 'shit' off my face and wash my hair.

"You look like a fucking peacock!" he said.

After I'd had a bath and washed my hair, Mr Cadman called me to his office. I was in two minds whether or not to ignore him, but Miss told me to go.

"You don't want to be in trouble again" she said.

Walking over to the main house, I was petrified that Mr Cadman was going to shout and holler at me, so when I knocked on the door, I was trembling. When I walked in, I had to stand up straight, waiting for him to turn round in that swivel chair. When he did, he asked for my hands like the other time and said, "Haven't I looked after you from the age of four, carried you in my arms over to the annexe because you were scared of the bats flying around and frightened of the dark? I also saved you from the fire. And didn't I take you back when you had nowhere else to go?"

"Yes sir."

He carried on then, saying repulsive things, like asking me if I loved my boyfriend. I replied "No sir."

Then he asked me, "Do you love me?"

I didn't answer him. Then he got up and pulled me towards him, asking me if my boyfriend was a nice kisser. He was so close that his spit was going in my face. I pulled my face away, but he grabbed my hair and started kissing me and at the same time, mauling me. I started kicking and struggling and managed to get away. I ran over to the annexe, terrified out of my life that this was happening to me all over again.

Then in the early hours of the morning, Mr Cadman came sneaking through to my bedroom. He tried to interfere with me, but again I managed to scare him off. The next day, before going to work, I asked Miss if I could go back to sleeping in the dormitory. At first, she was a little bit apprehensive, but Miss being Miss, she said yes in the end.

At work I kept silent all day, which caused an atmosphere in the shop. I did not know what to do and who to tell, knowing what had happened before, being interrogated by the Authority and feeling rejected when there was no justification.

Mrs Hoffman gave me a lift back to the orphanage.

"Life isn't always a bunch of roses" she said. "You have to take the good with the bad. Your life at the moment is full of ups and downs, but you will eventually get back on an even keel."

I was devastated knowing this was the last time I would be seeing Mrs Hoffman; it brought tears to my eyes. I had been so happy working in the salon, and it gave me hope and determination to succeed in the future.

I had made my mind up that if Mr Cadman was going to be mauling and slobbering over me and couldn't leave me alone, I just had to go away. That night, Miss had moved my belonging to the dormitory and when she turned the lights down low and the other girls were asleep, I got out of bed, put all the lockers in front of the door so that no one could get in or out, and stayed awake all night. All of a sudden, I heard Mr Cadman creeping passed the dormitory to the room I had occupied in the alcove, where another other girl was now sleeping. Then all hell broke out. The girl was screaming, yelling that there was a man in her room, and Miss had to calm her down. I jumped out of bed quickly to move the lockers back, and I

CHAPTER EIGHT

heard Mr Cadman shutting the back door. Miss told the girl she must have had a nightmare and told her to go back to sleep.

I knew that the next day I would have to leave. I knew that Mr Cadman would be looking for revenge and that I was in a dangerous situation. But no one was going to abuse me any more!

With the money I had saved over the weeks and months for my new flat, I knew I had enough for a train fare and bed and breakfast accommodation. I had already packed my belongings and was all set to go the next morning.

When morning came, I was trembling with fear from top to toe, knowing I could bump into Mr Cadman. As I walked over to the main house, I dumped my belongings into a bush, all ready to collect on my way out. When I saw Matron, I gave one big sigh of relief, and as soon as I had finished my breakfast, I was up and away. Scotland here I come, I thought.

I set off on my journey, catching the double-decker bus to Watford train station, then a train to London. I had to get another ticket for Scotland, which caused some difficulties because I wasn't precise in asking the ticket man exactly which station I wanted. In the end, he named some stations and I chose Edinburgh, which was a straight through train, all the way.

As the train pulled away, I was so excited that I forgot about all my cares and woes. I was free as bird. Looking at the scenery, watching the horses grazing in the fields and seeing the big barges going along the canal, it was as if I was in paradise.

After a while, I began to feel tired and fell into a deep sleep. The train master had to wake me up, saying we had arrived in Edinburgh. When I looked out of the window, the sky was pitch black and my nerves started getting the better of me. I felt as if I was having a panic attack. Then a man and a woman came up to me and asked if my name was Ingrid Williams. They were plain-clothes police officers,

CHAPTER EIGHT

sent to find me and escort me all the way back to London, where my guardian would be waiting for me, to take me back to the orphanage.

Miss Gisborne was dumbfounded. She had been very alarmed and was angry. "What possessed you to do such a thing?" she said. "I would like an explanation now!"

I didn't answer her. She could have talked to me until she was blue in the face, because I had no intention of talking to anyone or going back to the orphanage. All that was buzzing round in my head was that as soon as she stopped the car I was going to do a runner. Which I did.

I knew that no one would catch me; I could run as fast as the wind. I ran all the way down across the fields to the Watford bypass, where I hitched a lift from a lorry driver. I felt strange and a bit apprehensive. I had visions that the lorry diver might murder me, so I kept a low profile and let him do all the talking, but he turned out to be a 'good citizen' and dropped me off at the police station.

I was back to square one and again waiting for my guardian to take me back to the orphanage. This time, unknown to me, she had locked the car doors. When we arrived at the orphanage, all the staff were waiting for me. Two of the male staff took hold of me and I started to struggle, and then I saw Mr Cadman and went berserk. He dragged me along the floor to the staff sitting room, next to the fireplace, where he started beating the shit out of me.

I grabbed him and started beating the living daylights out of him, for all the years of malice, demoralisation and abuse.

A member of staff who was behind me snatched the poker out of my hands and Mr Cadman sat on me, pinning me down. He pressed so hard on the back of my neck that I started going dizzy. I could not stop shaking. Eventually I got to the point where I had collapsed and was completely knocked out.

Then all hell broke out. No one could bring me round at first and

CHAPTER EIGHT

when I did come to my sense, a doctor was next to me. He asked me to take a tablet, which made me feel woozy.

When I came round properly, I was in a cell at the police station in Ealing. Two plain-clothes police came to see me, and when they spoke in an understanding manner, I broke down in tears, telling them what had happened to me concerning Mr Cadman.

The policewoman explained to me in great detail that because I had tried to hurt Mr Cadman I could not go back to the orphanage.

"The Authorities are trying to find you a nice home" she said.

Then another police officer explained that I was being transferred under Government regulations.

"They have stipulated that you have to go to a girls' borstal, pending a court hearing" she said.

I asked her if I was going to prison because I had picked up a poker against my abuser. She replied, "No, you're not going to prison." She chose to ignore the rest of my question.

Chapter Nine

BORSTAL

I was taken away by two police officers in a black maria. When we reached the borstal, I was handed over to the warden, who explained the rules and regulations. Then I was handed over to other officers who searched me for sharp objects and looked through my hair. They gave me a blue jump-suit and a pair of plimsolls to wear.

I was then taken to the recreation room, where I saw the other girls. I seemed to be the youngest there, and when some of the others came to speak to me, one of the officers moved them on. I felt as though I was being segregated. Even the officer who was sitting with me made no conversation and when I asked some questions, everyone was quite adamant that they would not discuss with me the reason why I was there.

In the late afternoon the officers unlocked the doors and we were all escorted, two by two, to the toilets and the washroom. When everyone had finished, the officer went round counting us. Then we were led to the dining room.

After dinner and chores were done, we were escorted to the quiet room for one hour of television and one cigarette each. After that, we were escorted again, this time to the washroom and to be counted. Then all of us were taken to our cells for the night.

All day, everyday, the conversation was zilch. This didn't bother me as I was used to being in silence. Also, being in a cell on my own, not sharing, was no hardship as I had been locked in a room on my own, at times, from the age of six.

Being in that cell made me ponder on my past life. I thought about

CHAPTER NINE

the possessions I had: my blue stone bracelet, which I cherished; the little white bible with the gold cross; and the solid silver horse and carriage and my premium bonds, which had vanished into thin air. All the money I had saved for my flat, to enable me to get hold of my file and my birth certificate and to find my parents had gone. My plans had gone to wrack and ruin, all because a dirty old man in his sixties, thought he could carry on abusing me.

I had run away, forfeiting my job. The most famous hairdresser in the United Kingdom had transformed me from a country bumpkin into a beautiful young teenager. And now, here I was, sitting in a cell, all bedraggled and traumatized.

I tried to figure out what had happened. My birthdays had been virtually non-existent. I had usually only got one small item, and that was from the orphan fund, from the police station, but my seventh birthday had been sensational. Every year just before Christmas, a photographer took a photo of me to put in the newspaper, for people to buy me presents. Many times, it would be a plastic tea set.

I have never possessed any photographs of myself; not of when I was a baby, nor in my youth. I only saw the photograph in the newspaper once, and was told that it had to go into my file for future reference.

One particular Christmas, I had so many presents I was overwhelmed. It seemed too good to be true, and the presents came all the way from Jersey. Another time at Christmas, I had the most fantastic time in my life, riding a horse at Billy Smart's circus. It was magnificent. In the future, Billy Smart and Jersey would prove to have a connection with each other and with me.

Then I had had the major shock of my life. My name was Sheila Williams for nearly ten years, then it was changed to Ingrid Naylor, then it was Ingrid Williams, and when I lived at Windsor, it was Sheila Williams again. Then three years later, I was told I had a

CHAPTER NINE

middle name, Emilia. For one week, in the future, again I would be called Sheila.

At school I had never absconded, but when I had any burns or marks on my body, I was not allowed to go. Each time this had happened, the excuse to the teacher had been that I had tonsillitis. I know I used to have tonsillitis, every time my body could not take any more of being ill-treated. And it was so bad that I had to have a doctor.

I could not fathom out why no one could tell me the truth about what had happened to me, all the stuff in the secret file. It was like a jigsaw puzzle, with so many pieces missing. Lying in my bed in that cell, you couldn't hear a pin drop. There was complete silence. But my memory served me well and bits of the missing jigsaw started to flash back into my mind, including some things I had forgotten.

I clearly remembered one particular priest from St Peter's Church, when I was about six years old. The priest would come every now and again to have tea with us at the orphanage. He was a tall, very thin man and had black hair parted at one side and swept across his forehead. Every time he saw me, he would ruffle my hair and say, "God bless you, my child." I remember this man so well not because he was a priest, but because he sat opposite me at the table and I couldn't stop staring at him as he had a repulsive 'Adam's apple'. Every time he swallowed his food, that big lump would stick out like a gob-stopper. It was absolutely revolting! All the other priests I had known, from all the other churches, all seemed the same, with no distinctive features.

However, I had lost my faith. I had been praying at night to my Heavenly Father for help, when he was only a bogey man who just didn't exist. Matron, in the orphanage, always told me that I had a Heavenly Father, and when my rag doll was burnt, she had told me that angels would guard me. I had truly believed that God loved me, no matter what, and would never leave me, but it must have been just a fairytale.

CHAPTER NINE

I also recalled an incident which I did not want to remember, but it was buried in my brain. One day when I was between five and six years old, some kids were running rings round me, shouting and pointing their fingers in my face. Then one boy shouted at me, "Sheila Williams' daddy is going to be hanged tomorrow!" Then they all joined in the chant. I had tried to lash out in anger, but my head was spinning with frustration and I fell to the ground. Members of staff came over to see what the commotion was about, and I remember Matron cuddling me in her arms and saying, "Yes, there is a man who is going to be hanged, but it is not your daddy."

Other things came into my mind, from before the time when the lady had taken me away, aged four. There was a rickety old house on the top of a cliff. I was walking along towards the cliff, wheeling a small doll's pram, I heard people in the distance screaming at me and saw a woman running towards me waving her arms and shouting at me. I was standing right on the cliff edge. I could not recall the woman and I could not remember calling anyone mummy or daddy.

I remembered a night when a black cat jumped on my bed while I was asleep, waking me up in such a fright that I was screaming.

I remembered looking at a picture book every night before going to sleep. It was called Pussy Willow. I could not remember any other children being there.

All these things were going through my head as I cried myself to sleep in that cell every night.

The next day was similar as far as the routine was concerned. We had our breakfast, did some chores, and went outside in the yard for exercise. In the afternoon, we went to the recreation room and the occupational therapist lady asked me if I would like to make a patchwork quilt. "We can do it together" she said. "Yes please, miss" I replied.

"First, we have to sort out all the material."

CHAPTER NINE

When she brought out bags of material, I immediately thought of the gipsies riding their horses in exchange for bags of rags which they never received.

The occupational therapist took me under her wing; she showed me how to cut the material into fifty-pence piece shapes and to cut the cardboard identically to go between the materials, to make it stiff. I felt more at ease, being with Miss. She made conversation and cracked the odd joke here and there. We spent all afternoon just cutting up the material. When it was time for her to go home, she explained, "I'll be back on Monday, and if I'm allowed I'll bring in some magazines. Keep your chin up!"

The weekend hit me very hard. I broke down in floods of tears, knowing that the other girls were having visitors. All week no one had been to see me from the outside world. My guardian, it seemed, had abandoned me.

One of the officers saw me in tears and took me back to my cell. She took the time to speak to me, saying, "It won't be long now, you'll be leaving soon. Everyone is trying to find you a nice home, so just hang on." Those few kind words gave me back my self-esteem and a little hope.

On Sunday evening, the nice officer let me mingle in with the other girls, and instead of having only one cigarette, she let us all have two. Then we all sat down to play Monopoly. I had never played this game before, but the other girls were falling over themselves to help me and the officer let us play on until the game was finished.

Monday afternoon came, and I was over the moon when I saw the occupational therapist. She had kept her promise. She gave me some magazines and had sneaked in a bar of chocolate. I told her what had happened over the weekend, that I had broken down in floods of tears, and how the nice officer had supported me. We both carried on with the patchwork quilt and started sewing the patches together.

CHAPTER NINE

While I was sewing, I was reminiscing about the past and thinking that all the different colours represented all the people that had looked after me, from the age of four years.

Doing that patchwork quilt help me to occupy my mind. It also helped me to unlock some of the secret memories of the past, but all I wanted was someone to enlighten me, to tell me what was going to happen to me.

Every day the warden would do her usual rounds, say hello and goodbye and walked away merrily. However, this time she pulled up a chair and sat between the occupational therapist and me. She remarked how lovely all the colours blended in the patchwork quilt, but she was blind to what they all represented.

I knew in my heart that the warden did not just happen to sit down to have a chit-chat over a patchwork quilt. The real reason was to tell me that I was leaving in the morning.

"You'll be escorted back to Ealing police station" she told me, and she said goodbye.

The occupational therapist had a beautiful smile. She put her arms around me and gave me a big cuddle.

"When you go to court, you tell everyone what really happened in that orphanage" she said.

I was escorted back to my cell and given back my own tatty clothes to wear for the next day, for going to court.

That night seemed like an eternity. I was tossing and turning and pacing the cell floor, remembering the first time I had been in that police cell, half drugged after the doctor at the orphanage had virtually pushed tablets down my throat. When I had come round in that cell I had gone berserk, banging the cell bars with my shoe and shouting constantly "Let me out of here!" I had banged so hard in my rage that the heel of my shoe had come off. I had had to be restrained by the police officers until I had calmed down. The borstal people

CHAPTER NINE

had my shoe mended, but what they did not do was mend my shattered heart.

Chapter Ten

THE MENTAL HOSPITAL

I was taken back to Ealing police station the next day and escorted into the same cell that I had been in before. How did I feel? Traumatised. Minutes seemed like hours. I could hear two men nattering outside, then a smartly dressed, well-spoken one came into my cell. I was oblivious to what he was talking about; it was just a load of gobbledegook to me. As he was leaving, he turned round and said: "See you in court. It could be best all round if you kept your mouth shut, then we'll find you a nice home."

I was shell shocked that this man who was talking to me with his posh voice could be so cruel.

Soon after this, I was escorted by a policewoman into court. Hallelujah! Everyone in court seemed to have my file under their arm; the story about a girl named Sheila. I was terrified of what was going on around me. I saw Miss Gisborne, and she kept looking at me and smiling. Then I saw Mr Cadman, my abuser, ready to crucify me. My heart was beating so fast and my eyes filled with tears, but I was trying very hard not to let the tears fall from my eyes. I had a terrible fear inside me and my instinct was to run.

Everyone in court was talking to one particular man who then spoke to me. He was interrupted, however, by the man who had come to see me in the cell. With long and short pauses, eventually the main man explained to me that I needed a home where I could settle down and have a good, responsible life. "It has been decided that you are going to live with Dr Schultz and his family. He has beautiful gardens and a tennis court."

CHAPTER TEN

"Thank you, sir" I replied.

Two women, both somewhat on the large size, led me out of the courtroom. My guardian gave me a cuddle and said she was going to follow in her car. While I was being driven along, I became suspicious. These two women made just a few remarks to me, and normally, I always sat in my guardian's car. I was getting the urge to run. But where to?

I had been beaten with the cane so many times. I had a broken nose, my leg had been split open, I'd had broken ribs, been dragged along the floor by my hair, had burns on my body and been slapped around the head so many times that it felt as though my head would drop off. In the end, you start to retaliate, with grave consequences. So, who cared about two bitch women? But I wanted a nice home, so I kept my mouth shut. I had to reassure myself by looking out of the back window to make sure my guardian was behind.

As we drove through some woods, I couldn't see Miss Gisborne's car any more, and the two porkies in front were beginning to piss me off. I could see one of them looking at me through the rear view mirror, and then she started to accelerate the car, deliberately aiming to lose my guardian, which they did.

The car slowed down and we approached a big red barrier. The woman driver spoke briefly to a man and the barrier went up. She drove up a long driveway, then circled round to a big house with beautiful gardens. She spoke briefly again to another man, and then we drove along another driveway with what looked like concrete huts on each side. I couldn't see anybody walking around. The car finally stopped at the end of the drive, outside one of these concrete huts, and I was asked to get out of the car. I had never felt so terrified in my life as I did when I saw the handcuffs dangling from her belt.

I flatly refused to get out of the car. I felt as though my whole body was on fire and started screaming out, "I want my guardian! Where is

CHAPTER TEN

my guardian? I want my guardian!" I saw some other people running towards the car, and then Miss Gisborne drove up. She sat in the back of the car, trying to pacify me by saying, "Just come with me calmly. I will never leave you, no matter what."

We walked towards the main door and the woman who had driven the car unlocked it while the other bitch woman was restraining me, holding my arm very tight. As we walked in and I looked in front of me, I had a horrific shock. Damnation! I was on another planet for misfits. My guardian was crying, saying, "I'm sorry, I didn't know!"

It was a mental hospital, and I was in the ward for child misfits. Miss Gisborne was escorted to the door. A hospital sister walked me through the ward and said, "There is nowhere to run. All the doors are locked." She showed me my bed and pulled the curtains round.

I cried myself to sleep, thinking that the only person I truly trusted, my guardian, had deserted me. She knew that this wasn't because of a crime of mine. I had just turned fifteen and had been abused for years.

I woke up in a daze, thinking that all that had happened to me was just a dream. But reality set in when I heard the monkey noises and screaming going on. I was given some toiletries and shown to the toilet area: four sinks and four toilets with no doors, just partitions. The odour was so bad it made me retch. The smell lingered through the ward, where I was given my breakfast, a bowl of cornflakes, surrounded by the insane kids with snotty noses and drooling round the mouth. I couldn't stop heaving, so the ward sister took me to a small kitchen off the ward where she talked to me.

I spent most of my days in what they called an interview room. The sister had had a tip-off that Matron was on her way to the children's ward, and it was obvious she was coming to see me. She introduced herself as Matron Jenkins and only said nice things about me. She brought me a small bundle of magazines and a mixed bag containing cigarettes and a selection of beautiful fragrance toiletries.

CHAPTER TEN

The Matron and Sister asked me to join them in their ward round, but I was apprehensive of what monsters I would see. Matron knew all the patients' names. She made an old joke or two, then explained all the patients' disfigurements, which left them powerless.

We walked over to the other side of the ward, where there were baby's cots. Where I was expecting to see a little baby, I was horrified to see a big head and a tiny body. Matron saw the expression on my face and said that all these children were to be pitied, but I should be assertive. So much sadness, with my own pain, overwhelmed me. I just burst into tears. Before Matron went, she asked me to help Sister on the ward, and told me that my guardian was coming.

At night, I had my own routine with my bed. I would make sure that one side was tucked in tightly. With the other side, I would twist the sheet into a roly poly, then jump into bed, lift the mattress and tuck the roly poly underneath. Next, I would get hold of my long hair, twist it round my finger and bring it round in front of my neck. That was how it had to be so that no one could get to my 'privates' or pull my hair. Unknown to me, the nurse had been watching me do all this and reported me to the Sister.

The following day Sister called me in to her office. A doctor shook my hand and said hello. I was nervous about the questions I was going to be asked.

"It has been reported to us about your special bed making" said the Sister. "No one is going to touch you. How long have you been doing this?"

"Long time."

"Do you want to talk about it?"

My lips started to quiver and tears were running down my face. I shook my head, meaning no.

I stayed in the interview room, reminiscing about what had happened to me, sobbing. Sister put her arms round me before going home.

CHAPTER TEN

That night I didn't attend to my bed, but I felt out of my comfort zone and found it hard to go to sleep.

The next day Sister asked me to help the two nurses on the ward. I didn't like them. They were foreigners and half the time spoke in their own language, as well as screaming at the kids.

I was told to wash Janet, the baby in the cot. I'm sure they asked me to do this to get a laugh out of me. I was frightened, and they knew it. "She won't bite you!" said one nurse.

Before starting, I sprinkled lavender water round my nose to stop myself from heaving. I looked down, but that big head made me scared even to touch her. I didn't mind doing the little body, tiny fingers and toes. It took me ages to wash her and I could not quite get the hang of the nappy. I cleared up all my stuff, then Janet started to make gaga noises. The nurse said, "Janet is saying 'Thank you'." I bent over the cot and gave her a big smile. For nearly two weeks I washed Janet. I got quicker, so I was able to wash and dress some of the other children.

I was beginning to get frustrated with the way the other two nurses were treating the children, especially when Sister was off duty. The screaming, the way they shoved food down their mouths, and tablet time. It was a major stress listening to the sound of kids choking. I had the urge to get up and express my feelings. I wanted to help these children, who had no good life expectancy. I just wanted to show them some kindness.

I was told to go to Sister's office again and this time, Miss Gisborne was sitting there. I had a big grin on my face and she got up and gave me a big cuddle. I could only accept a cuddle for a second though, no kissing or touching my hair. These were no-go areas. Sister explained that I was being transferred to another ward where the patients would be much older, but the doors were not locked. And there was a padded room to restrain patients!

CHAPTER TEN

"We know you don't trust anyone, Ingrid, but now, we have to trust you not to run away" she said.

Miss Gisborne helped me to collect my bits and bobs. She had brought my own clothes, thank God, so I did not have to wear that V-neck smock anymore. I said my goodbyes, and Sister said, "Come up and see us, Ingrid! Off you go now, your guardian will take you."

When we got outside, it was heaven to breathe and smell the air, to listen to the birds singing in the trees, to see other people walking about, even though they were crazy misfits. As we were walking towards my new ward, Miss Gisborne seemed apprehensive. She was talking nineteen to the dozen. I think she thought I was going to do a runner. I bet she had her fingers crossed and was saying a prayer.

The ward sister asked us both to sit down. She said she was busy, but wouldn't be a minute. She looked fierce, her hair cropped short and going grey round the edges, and she spoke in an aggressive way. She walked hyper-fast through the ward and you could hear the keys jangling in her pocket.

The ward was half empty. The patients were elderly. One woman was constantly rocking in her chair, another was talking and scrawling in front of the wall, some were strapped into their chairs and others were just talking to themselves. All had clearly lost their marbles.

Miss Gisborne could see the downcast look on my face. I was thinking, "How long am I going to stay in this hell?"

The Sister took us into her office and explained the rules. She said I would be going to work every day in the sewing room with the other patients. She showed us the sleeping quarters; a four-bed room with my bed next to the door, thank God.

Miss Gisborne helped me to unpack my stuff, then she sat on the bed and showed me an article from the newspaper about when I was in court. She read it out. It said: "Fifteen year old sent to a mental hospital, Harperbury. She had nowhere to live, so they put her in a

CHAPTER TEN

hole." She asked me to bear with her until she could find me a home.

The Sister said that if I had any valuables, money or cigarettes, they would be locked in the office, as other patients went scavenging through the lockers, bags, and dustbins because of their illness.

When my guardian left I felt empty inside, so I walked over to the dining room and sat next to the window. I saw a very tall woman walking round and round the patio square. She must have been in her forties, and she was wearing a big pink bow hair slide, with a fag hanging from her mouth and a bag screwed under her arm. When I looked down at her feet, I saw she had lock-up boots on.

At four o'clock that afternoon, the other patients returned to the ward from the sewing and laundry rooms. Out of them all, there were only two who spoke and looked normal: their names were Ann Barrett and Caroline Bash. We all sat at the same table, including the woman with the lock-up boots.

I found myself peering at her. It was that big pink bow in her hair. It was so ridiculous. We all slept in the same dormitory as well, and after tea, the four of us retired there.

Ann introduced me to the woman in the lock-up boots. "Joan is her name. She's harmless until she's provoked, then run! She has the strength of a horse and it takes four strapping men to hold her down. Usually it happens when other patients steal her junk. That's the reason she's with us."

She carried on to say that Joan had been sent there 20 years ago for quarantine. She had had tuberculosis and had to be isolated, but she had been there ever since. Twenty years! I was gobsmacked. So sad too. Who had the right to take a person's life away?

Ann carried on telling me about the sort of patients who stayed there - Downs syndrome, lesbians and gays, manic schizophrenics. It was a stepping-stone to Rampton Hospital for the criminally insane. Caroline said she had heard stories about Rampton. "It don't matter if you're young or old, you'll have an early grave, the way you are treated" she said.

I was horrified. I was only fifteen and didn't understand this vocabulary, nor did I know that any of these places existed.

The other sister came on duty, and she was the opposite of the previous one. She was clumsy and had a nice smile. We all had hot drinks and the lights went down. I was frightened and kept bobbing my head up, looking over to Joan to make sure she was still in bed. The night nurse reassures me that Joan had had a 'cocktail' and would sleep like a baby.

The next day we all walked, or should I say shuffled, along the drive. I saw the chain link fence and it looked inviting. Then we all went our separate ways: Caroline went to the laundry and Ann went another way, to Matron Jenkins's flat. She had not told me she was Matron's cleaner, and after I had been discussing with her what happened on the children's ward, I felt just a bit wary.

I went to the sewing room with some others, where there were also some women employees from outside. I was shown to my place, right next to the window, and introduced to my mentor. She gave me a pile of sheets to hem in my coffee break.

I sat on my own by the window, and lo and behold, come rain or shine, I would see Joan with her lock-up boots, fag hanging from her mouth. Bless her! "If only she doesn't hit me!" I thought. I glanced over to look out of the opposite window, and in the distance I could see some male patients, all dressed in white, in a crocodile line with male nurses. I stretched my neck to see more, but they had disappeared.

In the afternoon, it was discussion and free time. Discussion time was just a load of people squabbling among themselves. Free time was dancing, with lots of hand clapping. To see the gleam on the patients' faces overwhelmed me.

The next day, a woman from outside came and sat with me on our

CHAPTER TEN

coffee break. She told me more about Joan. "Do you know that there were over fifty men and women with TB sent here for isolation?" she said. "Some died and the rest stayed here. It was diabolical, what they did here." She told me about young girls who were sent here pregnant, had their babies, and then the babies were taken away. Two of those women still remained even now, without their babies, after about fourteen years. She did not tell me their names.

During the afternoon I saw the male patients shuffling along again. Some looked disfigured and crippled. I got up, went over to the window, and waved at them and blew kisses. The whole sewing room was in fits, laughing, but I couldn't understand why, because it was not that funny. The woman in charge came up to me and said, "Those men can't wave back to you, they're all in straitjackets. You can make some on your sewing machine."

I was stunned at this statement. There are no words to describe my feelings.

Walking back to the ward with my buddies and seeing that chain link fence, it looked more appealing than ever. My days were doom and gloom.

In the evening, I sat with Sister in her office and burst into tears. I couldn't hold them back, but I did not want my buddies to see me cry. The Sister gathered that I'd had a bad day in the sewing room, and said I would not be going back there any more. She told me that the next day I would be going to have my photograph taken. "You can refuse, but it looks better on paper if you don't" she said.

I told Caroline and Ann about having my photo taken. They said that if you refuse, you get sent to Rampton hospital. I thought they were just putting the fear of God in me, knowing I was naive.

The next morning I helped Sister make the beds, and then was told to walk over to the hall and wait in the waiting room. Someone would call me.

CHAPTER TEN

Dr Schultz called me in and there were six other doctors there. They all said hello, then I was asked to stand behind a chalk line and to strip off my clothes. I was shaking. Standing naked, I put one hand across my breasts and the other over my privates. I was told to put my hands down by my side and turn round slowly while a man photographed me.

When I got back to the ward, I felt degraded, dirty and sick to the stomach. I could not eat or speak. The Downs syndrome patients, who I called my buddies, tried to comfort me. Matron came to see me, but I couldn't speak; I just turned my head away.

"I want you to go to the children's ward to work over the weekend" she said. "Walk freely, sit outside and have your cigarette, or whatever. On Monday, be at my quarters ten o'clock sharp."

She walked away, leaving a carrier bag full of bits and bobs for me.

I went up to the children's ward and when Sister unlocked the door, all the children were surprised to see me. I looked into the cot, and Janet's eyes sparkled. She had a big smile on her face and was speaking her gaga noises. I washed her, and got the nappy right this time. Then at dinner time, I helped to do the feeding. In the afternoon, we had the wireless on and just fooled around, playing games. It was a fun day, and the following day, Sunday, was the same.

On the Monday I was at Matron's flat dead on time. Her flat was beautiful. Matron realised I was nervous and smiled at me, then explained to me that she did not want me in the ward during the day, only at night, and at weekends I would work in the children's ward. She handed me some new clothes: two white blouses, a black skirt, a pair of black patent leather shoes, two pairs of stockings with seams and a pair of white cotton gloves.

I was over the moon. All these brand new clothes for me! But I was baffled about the white gloves. Matron looked at me and said, "You wear the gloves when you put the stockings on, so that you don't

CHAPTER TEN

ladder them. Your new job is waitress to the doctors, in the main house. You will have all your meals there. Tony is going to teach you everything you need to know."

When I left Matron's flat, I was ecstatic and bursting with energy. I had seen so many shocking things. There was a patient who had bandages all round her arms and hands and had to be watched twenty-four hours a day. Then one day when I just happened to walk past, the patient had managed to remove the bandages and I saw she was covered in blood, all round her mouth: She was biting her own flesh. I had seen a patient being restrained, or to put it more plainly, being beaten up. I was deeply shocked, but after seeing and hearing these atrocities I had earned my freedom. I thought, "There is a God looking down on me!"

Back at the ward, Sister gave me a half-hearted grin. I wanted to tell the world, but I just stayed in the dormitory. Nothing here had changed: the constant bickering, screaming and kicking off.

I heard the gangs returning from work. Caroline and Ann seemed a bit off with me, but I just went along with the flow. I did not want anyone clouding my spirits. If the truth were known, I was the one who was envious; of Ann, cleaning Matron's flat. She went to St Albans to do errands, and could go out at weekends to do her own shopping.

The next day I looked the business, all booted and suited. I left the ward before the other patients went to work. Sister gave me a smile, and for her to smile, something must be good! As I was walking along the drive, I was being a bit swanky, flicking my hair and doing the odd twirl. As I got near to the main house, I waved to the security man at the barrier. I was just yards away from the outside world.

That day was a total disaster, yet it was also a real education. Tony had to teach me how to do silver service waitressing. I knew how to lay a table, but there were so many different kinds of cutlery and I did not know which went where. I had to learn how to fold a napkin into a pyramid, where to place the glasses and how to use the serving utensils, using two spoons in one hand, for vegetables and potatoes. It was so tricky. And the cheese board; I had to remember so many varieties. However, within two or three weeks I had mastered it to perfection. The food which the doctors and their guests ate was also my dinner, and it was like heaven!

The job gave me joy and stability, but inside, I was yearning so much to say my goodbyes to this place that I would never be able to forget. I did realise that it could destroy my life: the immoral things that might have been written about me, and the photographs of me naked. The day I was in court and advised to keep my mouth shut, I did not have any knowledge that the newspaper reporters were there. The Government officials hadn't wanted any scandal and they knew that I was here because of the head of the orphanage's crime. They just wanted me to vanish into thin air. What Government stamp had been put on my file?

I tried not to think about that devilish thing, but I felt that one day the jigsaw would be completed. And what about the other poor bastards who were here? What were their crimes? Having TB?

Miss Gisborne came every week without fail. I did have one other visitor, but she made me feel bad about myself; my ex foster mother, Ann Naylor. I asked how she had known I was there, and she said she had read the article in the newspaper. I asked if my name had been mentioned, but she said it had not been. It had just said I was fifteen and from Hawkridge orphanage.

She carried on to say that Pop had died. Even though he pissed his pants and was constantly knocking that dirty, smelly pipe against the fireplace, I had thought the world of him. I never saw Mrs Naylor again.

I asked Miss Gisborne about Christmas, but she seemed a little bit

CHAPTER TEN

vague. I began to feel frustrated, as it was not far away. I began to get emotionally upset. Christmas: baby Jesus, angels, gold, frankincense and myrrh? Welcome to Christmas at the funny farm!

I was not upset about mums and dads or presents, it was just having to be there. No doctors' meetings, no work, some patients going home. Christmas could be any other day; if the world was coming to an end, bombs were dropping or there was an earthquake, Joan would still have a fag hanging from her mouth, walking round and round that fucking pavement in her lock-up boots. Others would still be rocking in their chairs, nodding their heads and talking to the walls.

I decided to ask the nice sister if I could work in the children's ward over Christmas, but she said I would have to ask the other sister, who was in charge. It took me days to pluck up the courage, and then when I did, it was only to be told I would have to ask Matron.

Every evening I used to take a paper bag from the cleaner's trolley and take it with me to work. It was a doggy bag for cakes and leftovers from the doctors' meetings, which I took back to the ward. When the lights went down in the dormitory, we had our 'take away', scoffing cream cakes. When we looked at Joan, she would have dollops of cream all round her dirty black beard, and we all had to hide under the bedclothes, in stitches.

One particular evening, on my way back to the dormitory, I walked smack bang into Matron and Miss Gisborne and was told to go to the office. I knew I would be in big trouble. My heart was pounding as I shoved the paper bag into Ann's hands. However, when I came out of the office, I was exhilarated. I was going to Windsor for Christmas!

I could not sleep, and in the morning, I was droopy eyed. I was just leaving the dormitory when Sister asked me where I was going. "It's Saturday. I'm going to the children's ward" I replied.

"No, not today. You can go out with Ann to St Albans."

CHAPTER TEN

"Do you mean me, Sister?"

"Yes, and you can pick up the money which your guardian left for you."

I could not believe what was happening. Two miracles! It was amazing to be actually going out, without bunking over the fence. I was in my element.

That was one fabulous day, looking round the shops and going to an Indian restaurant. Ann was my chaperone and she loved it too. We walked passed St. Albans Cathedral, which brought back memories of singing in the gallery there, in the choir.

I had felt sorry for Joan as I went out. She would be in the dormitory on her own over Christmas, so I went into a cake shop and bought her a Victoria sandwich cake, filled with jam and cream, and got her some new slides for her hair. As we walked to the bus stop, we passed an old tramp and I gave him some money I had left over. He shouted after us, "You are beautiful!" Ann turned round, but the tramp shouted, "Not you, love, the other one!"

We were like two little kids, giggling all the way back.

But my excitement wore off. I couldn't sleep. How do you cure pain, anger, frustration, insecurity? What was I going to tell the other girls at Windsor about where I lived? What if Miss Darwell was still there? And what if Miss Burton started to call me Sheila again? I told Ann in confidence, knowing she was Matron's cleaner.

The big day arrived and I had butterflies in my stomach. I had to go and see Matron, who asked if I was excited, and I replied that I was. She said, "A little bird has been whispering in my ear. You have nothing to worry about. Miss Darwell has left Windsor, and you will be Miss Burton's guest."

She gave a gracious smile. "Sheila is a nice name" she said, sarcastically but in a nice way. "Yes, I like that name."

She gave me an envelope containing some money. "Call it the

CHAPTER TEN

doctors' tips. Buy yourself some cakes and a nice slide for your hair, and some new paper bags for the cleaners."

I burst out laughing. Even when we were driving along to Windsor, thinking about what Matron had said, I had little outbursts of laughing. She had known all along!

Chapter Eleven

CHRISTMAS IN WINDSOR

When I was travelling with my guardian she always drove half the way along the motorway and half along the back way through little villages, and we always stopped for tea and cakes. She was very particular about the tea shop, and I would know when we went there I was going to have one of her pep talks.

When we reached Windsor I became agitated, so she drove round the outskirts to steady my nerves. As we drove up to the house Miss Burton was there to greet us, and I saw some girls peering through the windows. It was a wonderful moment, seeing Jane Burton again. She kept on saying, "Haven't you grown into a beautiful girl, with your lovely hair." She gave me lots of cuddles.

I was introduced to the other girls. "This is Sheila" she said. Miss Gisborne and I looked at each other and laughed. My name for the next three weeks was Sheila. Miss Gisborne went with Miss Burton to the office, with my file under her arm, while I mingled with the other girls. When she left, she gave me a kiss on the cheek, and as usual, I wiped it off.

I was given my own bedroom. Miss Burton fussed over me and we had some lovely conversations.

The next day we went into Windsor town centre. We walked round the antique shops and the elegant boutiques and went to her favourite tea shop, right opposite the castle. We walked past my old school, Lady Mary's - it seemed very posh! When we got back, Miss Burton made me a snack, the same as she always had done, of chunky toasted bread with dripping, sprinkled with salt.

CHAPTER ELEVEN

The following day we walked along the river, as we had always watched the Eton college boys rowing, and went out with the other girls up the Long Walk to the Copper Horse.

On Christmas Eve Miss Burton and I and the other girls, went to midnight mass. When we walked into the church and I saw that big cross of Jesus hanging by chains from the ceiling, it hit me hard. Tears were streaming down my face, and Miss Burton held my hand tightly - in a nice way. The church looked magnificent, with candles glowing everywhere. The choir sang in Latin, sounding angelic, the priest sprinkled holy water around and the smell of frankincense was overwhelming. I will never forget that night.

Christmas Day, for once, was a beautiful day. Miss Burton bought me a rosary. If there was a sad moment, I blocked it out with blissfulness and contentment. However, I would have to pay the price of the devil, having to go back to the mental hospital.

Fifteen years later I went to see Miss Burton in the Isle of Man, and still she called me Sheila!

When I left after this Christmas holiday, I felt in deep pain. My guardian was talking constantly, but I was oblivious to what she was saying. All I wanted to do was run away, never to be seen again. But the sister on the children's ward had trusted me to come back. The doctors trusted me, Matron trusted me, and the sister with the grim smile who had made it all possible trusted me. Loyalty. Deep down inside I knew I had to go back.

I was feeling very disappointed. Miss Gisborne and I went straight to the sister's office, just for a general chat, but when I started to tell her about the midnight mass, I lost it. I was all shaken up inside and burst into tears. Trying to say thank you to Sister made matters worse.

Miss Gisborne put her hands on my face. "Be patient" she said. "I am going to find you a nice home."

After she left I was bombarded by my buddies, the Downs

CHAPTER ELEVEN

syndrome patients, shouting, "Ing, Ingram back!" They never called me Ingrid. Why they couldn't was a mystery, as the other patients, still in cuckoo land, could manage it.

Even Megan, who was tongue-tied and could only walk a few steps, crawled along the floor to greet me. I always felt uneasy being around Megan as she kept having fits. When she had a bad turn she would put her fists up to you and bang them against the wall. She had some white communication cards. She showed me the card which had a sad face on, then pointed her finger at me.

A nurse in the children's ward had told me that mad people show no pain or remorse, but I have heard their screams, heard them laugh, seen them crying and pleading when being held down to be injected with a tranquilliser or put in solitary confinement.

We had all returned from the Christmas period now, Caroline, Ann and me. We laughed and joked, told our tales. Joan had her glittery slides in her hair, and everything was back to normal in our dormitory.

The next day we all went back to work. Joan, come rain or shine, fag hanging out of her mouth, was walking round and round that square in her lock-up boots. The male patients in their straitjackets were walking round the grounds in a crocodile line. The freaky guards were there, eyeballing you. I was always a bit wary walking past them.

Being back at work gave me a boost. The doctors made some wisecracks, asking if I had visited the Queen, having been to Windsor. Ha ha!

On the Saturday Ann and I went to our favourite Indian restaurant in St. Albans, and then on Sunday I returned to the children's ward. I had such a lovely reception, it made me feel good about myself.

I was always told to be on my guard when walking round the grounds, so I was. I always walked in the middle of the drive, never near the bushes, and there was always someone else, like a member

CHAPTER ELEVEN

of staff, passing. One particular day, I was not feeling well so I left work early and took the short cut across the green. A big, big, mistake! As I was walking, I heard someone behind me and started to panic. I glanced behind me and saw a male patient dangling his arms in an irate way.

I was petrified and started to run as fast as I could. All I could see in front of me was the six-foot metal fence, and in desperation, I scrambled over, ripping my clothes. I had cuts on my knees, hands and face; blood everywhere. I was in a terrible state. A couple picked me up in their car and took me back to the hospital. I felt very ill. I couldn't speak, owing to the shock and my throat being sore. I was cold, shivering and frightened of what was going to happen to me.

Matron and Sister cleaned up my wounds, but that is all I can remember of this time. I went down with tonsillitis, drifting in and out of fever and not being aware of my surroundings. But then I was suddenly aware of a hypodermic needle in front of me. I went absolutely loopy, thrashing about the bed shouting, "Don't you dare give me that needle! Don't you dare!"

Then I felt something metallic in my hair. Again I went berserk, shouting "Take these fucking sputniks off my head!" I thought they were electrodes. I heard a sharp voice saying, "It is an antibiotic injection, and it is a clip in your hair, we're just clipping your hair up!"

The screen was taken away and I started to feel much better. Matron and Sister mollycoddled me. I was given jelly, ice-cream, custard and semolina with a big blob of jam: scrumptious! With my medicine, I had a spoonful of malt, tasting like honey toffee. It was absolutely beautiful.

Ann was in her element telling me that my guardian had been to see me, but I had been away with the fairies, and with all the things I had been saying, she could not stop laughing. However, it is not funny, to see with your own eyes a woman in her thirties lying in a bed, brain dead, a cabbage. She had had a lobotomy in her past that had been a cock up. A life taken away. I suppose all these sorts of things played on my mind.

These people were not what I had thought when I first encountered them. They were not misfits from another planet, nor were they devil demons. They were just human beings. I heard them scream, heard them laughing and heard their pleas. I saw them crying and expressing sadness and happiness.

Was this place to become a stigma for my life? I was never on any psychiatric treatment or medication, but what had they put in my file? Was it, "If you shut your mouth in court we'll find you a beautiful home"? or was it a naked photograph, exposing me for all to see?

When Miss Gisborne next, she was unusually bubbly. She was bursting to tell me she had found me a home. I was ecstatic - over the moon!

I was now as free as a bird to get my birth certificate and my file, but not yet, not just yet. I was on my way to my new home.

Chapter Twelve

THE TRUTH AT LAST

After I had said my farewells to everyone, Matron Jenkins escorted me to my Miss Gisborne's car. She smothered me with kisses and cuddles, but the truth was it meant nothing to me. It was all too late to bury the hatchet. All I wanted to do was to get into my guardian's car and go. The mental hospital never existed, it was all a terrible nightmare, to be hidden from people in the outside world. Only to be buried in my brain for the rest of my life.

Finally, we were on our way. We dove through the barriers.

Hit the road Jack, not coming back no more, no more, no more
Hit the road Jack, not coming back here no more.

I was in my element and I had a big grin on my face. Miss Gisborne suggested that we stop to have a bite to eat, as it was a long journey, but what she really meant was, she was going to give me another of her pep talks. As we got out of the car I pretended to do a runner, which frightened the life out of her. When she realised I was only joking we both walked into the café laughing. I just could not stop laughing, seeing the look on her face when she thought I was going to run away.

She started to explain all the gory details about the hostel.

"Mr and Mrs Dooley, who are both Irish, run the hostel, and the second person in charge is Miss Knapman. You're allowed to go out as you please as long you inform the person in charge. At night, you have to be back at the hostel by nine o'clock. If you do not return, the police will be informed."

CHAPTER TWELVE

She went on to say that she could not find me a job in hairdressing.

"We did manage to find you a job in a factory until an apprenticeship comes up in hairdressing" she said. "I know it isn't up to your expectations, but the money you earn will pay for your keep and any money left over is yours to do with as you please. At the hostel there are eight girls including yourself. One of the girls, Ruth, also works at the factory so you won't be on your own." She paused and looked straight into my eyes. I knew by the expression on her face she was about to tell me her woes.

"After today, I won't be seeing you any more as I have left my job with the authorities. You will not have a guardian any more. You will be completely on your own."

I was utterly dumbfounded. Tears came to my eyes. She had been so loyal to me in the end and stayed with me while I was in that hellhole. Now I was going to have to find my own destiny in life.

It took a while to settle down and get acquainted with everyone. Mrs Dooley took me under her wing and she would invite me to her private rooms, just for a general chit-chat. She told me all about Ireland and how there were horses roaming everywhere.

Even though she was laughing and joking with me, she was not well, as she had 'women's problems'. However, she always had a cigarette in her mouth and even had them sent to her all the way from Ireland. I distinctly remember that, because they were in a bright yellow packet; they must have been special Irish cigarettes.

Mr Dooley just stayed in the background, only saying hello and good-bye. I was never sure of Miss Knapman. She reminded me of Miss Darwell from Windsor, who had hit me with that copper stick, so I kept my distance from her. The other girls were too busy to notice me. They went out to work, then out in the evening with their boyfriends, and only said hello in passing.

CHAPTER TWELVE

Nevertheless, I made a friend in Ruth. I called her Ruthie. I had never had a black friend before. With her tiny face and massive afro hair-do, she could have been a model for the marmalade jar!

She showed me the ropes and all that was expected of me. She explained that doing any cleaning in the hostel was optional.

"Cook might ask someone to volunteer laying the tables or to help washing up" she said. "Breakfast time is just help yourself, but at the weekends you have a cooked breakfast. During the week, you take sandwiches to work and the evening meal is at six o'clock. If you work overtime, you just let cook know the day before, or you'll have no dinner saved.

"When you go into the dining room, there is no special place to sit. During the evenings, we go to the sitting room and watch TV. It is optional if you want to smoke, but at ten o'clock, it's a hot milky drink and biscuits, then bed."

The next day I was bursting with energy to go out with Ruthie. We wandered around Leytonstone High Street, where the market was full of people, waiting in endless queues. As we passed one stall, the market man shouted out to me, "Come and buy some of my cockles, my beautiful young lady!"

"No thank you sir" I said, shaking my head. Every one in the queues laughed at me for being so polite. "Come over here and give me a kiss!" he shouted. Then another man shouted, "Come on, gorgeous, buy some of my scrumptious apples!" and then he threw me one. I felt so happy, being the centre of attention.

We then made our way to the bowling alley, and my eyes lit up, "Yes, this is my game!" I said. As we walked in, some of the teenage boys started to wolf whistle at me and mutter among themselves.

We met up with Gloria, who also lived at the hostel, and her boyfriend Nick. She was nice, slim, with long wavy black hair and blue eyes. Some of her other friends joined us and it was all good fun.

CHAPTER TWELVE

It didn't matter if the ball went down the alley or you knocked all ten skittles down.

Nick drove us back to the hostel. Ruthie and I left Gloria to do her snogging in the car, while all we could hear was Miss Knapman being boorish in the background about us being ten minutes late.

Ruth went all silent on me, and not knowing what I had done wrong, I asked her. She replied, "Well, you are good looking, nice figure, and you are a bit quirky." Then she started to laugh, "And you speak funny."

"Well, thank you Ruth, that means we are still going to be friends."

Yes, I did lap up all the attention and I was in my element. I was like a little girl lost making up for lost time. However, at night, it was a different story; I would wake up in tears having had terrible dreams. But I couldn't tell anybody.

The next day, to round off the weekend, Gloria suggested we all go to Whipps Cross boating lake. Mick picked us up in his car and we were on our merry way. We hired two boats and just fooled around, splashing each other with the water. When the boatman saw us, he started to shout at us through his loudspeaker, telling us to bring in the boats. However, we took no notice of him, until he started to go mad. I was going hysterical. I just could not stop laughing all the way back to the hostel.

When Miss Knapman heard the hullabaloo, I'm sure she thought I was humiliating her in front off the other girls. When she spoke to me, I couldn't stop laughing in her face, and when she was walking away I could hear her muttering bad words about me. I had only been there for three days and I think I had made my first enemy. I knew I had to keep a still tongue because of my temper, and just walk away from anyone who was trying to antagonise me.

Mrs Dooley told another girl to ask me to report to her in her flat. I was a little bit anxious, thinking Miss Knapman had said I was being

CHAPTER TWELVE

rude, but when I got there, I was horrified. Mrs Dooley was sitting upright in the chair, bathing her breast. She had dreadful boils and she was squeezing them to get the pus out. She only had kind words to say to me.

The weekend was over and Ruth and I were getting ready to go to work. We made our sandwiches and were off. We caught the bus at the top of the road to Stratford and got off at the Rex Cinema. Then we crossed the road, walked round the Builders Arms Pub, and there was the Gatehills factory in front of us.

I had never worked in a factory before. I wasn't frightened of working hard; I was just nervous meeting new people. As we walk in, everyone was standing in a queue waiting to clock on. May, the forelady, gave me my clocking in card and showed me round the factory. She explained that the company made electrical items for Valor, the heating company. As we continued walking around, all eyes were on me. There was a mixture of people working there; young and old, whites and blacks. There was one particular family. There were four brothers, the older one was the manager, two sisters who did home work and the mother, the aunties and uncles worked for the firm too.

May, the forelady, was my mentor for the day. She was nice and fair. She showed me how to put the parts together for an electric fire when all the bits and pieces came down on a conveyor belt.

The atmosphere was not what I had expected. Music was playing and the older women were laughing and joking. The men walking past kept on asking, "a' right love?" The young girls were in a little clique being bitchy, but I did not care. I had no intention of staying here, in a dead end job. But it paid the rent.

Ruthie had met her black boyfriend and I met my new sweetheart at the factory, and all his family who worked there too. We did our courting in the pub. On Saturdays, all of us from the factory met up and went to Cooks' Pie and Mash shop.

CHAPTER TWELVE

I will never forget one particular time we went to the cinema. We bought two bags of prawns before going in, and sat in the back row. The film was called 17 and it was a French film about a young teenager boy's experience of puberty and his imagination running wild. I could not stop laughing, and when everyone else in the audience stopped it made me laugh even more. In fact I started to choke on the damn prawns! My boyfriend never took me to the cinema again after that.

One day we went on a picnic together. His mother had made a basket of goodies to eat. We biked out into the countryside, then walked up a big hill with tall grass, on a farmer's land. We kissed and frolicked around, but my imagination started to run wild, realizing that we had to walk down that hill and thinking about snakes slithering in the grass. The more I thought about that, the more anxious I became, so I insisted that my boyfriend give me a piggyback down the hill. It really was hilarious. He was holding the baskets and had me on his back. We never went on any more picnics either.

Time passed so quickly. Soon I had moved on, left the factory and the hostel and got a live-in job as a waitress-cum-cleaner in the doctors' quarters at Epping General Hospital. The housekeeper who was in charge was a bit of a stickler where the rules were concerned. The first rule: No boyfriends in your room. Second rule: No intoxicating drinks. Third rule: No shenanigans with the doctors!

She showed me around and explained the weekly rota; the days I would be working and the days I had off. She said that if there was a red cross in the square, you could put your name down for overtime. Then she showed me my room and gave me the key. It was a very poky room with just the bare necessities, situated above the main reception area. Every time you left the premises you had to sign an 'in/out' register, because of the fire regulations.

At first I felt a bit insecure, being on my own, but then there was

CHAPTER TWELVE

a knock on the door. It was the girl in the next room to me, who was also working for the doctors. Her name was Sineadh and she was Irish. She was small and dumpy, with shoulder-length brown hair, and she never wore any make-up. In fact she was quite ugly, but she had a happy-go-lucky attitude and did not give a monkeys about anyone or anything. We became friends.

I was happy doing my job. Because I was the youngest working there, the doctors gave me a nick-name, Poodle. The work, for me, was like water off a duck's back. I could not tell a soul that I had been waiting on doctors in that mental hospital. When anyone started to be nosey, I would snap at them.

There are certain incidents which stick in my mind. Sineadh had a brainwave; she wanted to go all beautiful and, knowing I had been a hairdresser, she asked me to do her hair. I started by making her face up and went over the top with the rouge. Then I did her hair. I pleated the back and back-combed the front into a bouffant, then Sineadh virtually sprayed a whole tin of lacquer on her hair.

When we went on duty, I just could not go into the dining room with Sineadh. I had to stay outside the door, pissing myself laughing. When the doctors saw Sineadh they were flabbergasted; she looked like Aunt Sally with all the rouge she had on her cheeks.

The housekeeper knew all the skulduggery we got up to. When we went out, she would inspect our rooms. She even knew we sneaked down late at night to raid the main kitchen for lots of goodies. The ticket man reported us to the hospital for jumping on trains and not paying our fares and then the two of us received a rollicking, big time.

My boyfriend decided to work nights at the factory to save some money to buy a car, and I worked all the overtime that was going. In fact, everything was going dandy - until I went down with tonsillitis again, and a fever.

CHAPTER TWELVE

The doctors were giving me injections all round the clock. I smacked the housekeeper in the mouth when all she had done was to provoke me when I was ill.

My boyfriend was sneaking in and out of my room, unknown to the housekeeper, until I got better. However, things didn't stay hunky-dory for long. I got the sack, because the housekeeper said she saw semen on my sheets.

Mr Dooley came to pick me up to take me back to the hostel. Miss Knapman was in her element being obnoxious towards me. I had no job and was feeling pretty low, but my friend Ruth was still there and tried to comfort me.

Mrs Dooley asked me to explain everything that had happened at the hospital, owing to me being sacked. I knew what she was up to; she wanted all the gory details to put in my file.

The next day I went job hunting - and the following day, and the day after that. I eventually got a job at Gracie's hair salon in Leytonstone, on a month's trial.

My boyfriend bought his first car, a Triumph Herald, and bought me an engagement ring. We were official now, a courting couple. I was over the moon. When I got back to the hostel, I was swanking around, putting my hand in front of everyone's noses. I also showed Mrs Dooley, and she was pleased for me. I stayed in her flat, helping her doing the boils on her breast, as she was not well. I suddenly knew then that I really wanted to become a nurse.

I asked Mrs Dooley how I could become a nurse, but when she replied she was laughing. "First you have to be able to read and be able to spell" she said. "And you have to be eighteen."

"Who will help me to learn to read and spell?"

"Well, you can go to night school or college, but it could take years, seeing as you are dyslexic."

What she really meant was that I had a mental block. I replied in a sarcastic way, "Well, when I've learnt to read and spell, I can write a story about my life."

Mrs Dooley did not reply to this. She got the strops and started to put all her stuff away. I must have hit the wrong button.

That night in bed my head was going all hazy, thinking how Mrs Dooley had turned on me when everything was okay. Even though I seemed contented, I had an irritating niggly feeling going on inside my head. I was always gullible, and I was just a punchbag. If anything went wrong, it was always 'Sheila Williams done it Miss!' because I had no family to tell. Now it was time to do something about it.

The next day was my day off from the hairdressers, so I decided to go to London on my own, to a place I had been thinking about for some time. I had not prayed or been to church recently and I did not have the audacity to ask for help; God had left me a long, long, time ago. So I made myself all glamorous, knowing that some kind gentleman would help a damsel in distress. I made up my lunch box and took the money I had stashed away, and I was on my way.

As I walked down the road to the station I was hoping I got on the right train. When I got to the station I was so nervous that I asked the ticket man in my tongue-tied way if he could help me to get to my destination. In fact he went out of his way, doing his very best to help me. He even drew a small diagram and showed me the platform where I had to get my train. Standing on that platform I was in a right pickle, but I got on the right train in the end and got off at the right station in London.

I must have asked about twenty pedestrians the way, showing them my piece of paper. I was walking down this street and that street, getting confused with my left and right, getting nowhere, so I sat on a bench eating my sandwich. I had given up the hunt. I sat there very downhearted, while other people came and sat on the bench.

Then a woman started to make conversation with me. I explained to her that I was lost and showed her my piece of paper. When she looked, she replied, "No, my dear, you are not lost. The building you are looking for is just up this road." I could not believe, at first, what she was telling me and I could not thank her enough. I carried on walking and then finally got to my destination. It was right in front of me; an oldie-worldie building.

Somerset House.

I waited outside for a while to get my thoughts together. I would have to hold my head up high and be assertive, but it did not happen like that when the receptionist asked if she could help me. I tried to explain, the best way I could, and she gave me a form to fill out. I was completely gutted because I just could not spell, and neither did I have any history about my parents.

A man came out from who knows where and took me to one side of the room. He asked me many questions, some of which I could not answer. I found myself talking about the orphanage, which unnerved me somewhat, then he filled in the form for me and gave it to the usher. This man told me to follow him into a massive room where there were other people sitting at long, antique-looking tables with green brass table lights. Everyone was reading or writing, and it was so quiet you could hear a pin drop.

The gentleman took me upstairs to the gallery and he told me, "I will try to help you, but I am not making any promises. Luck is on your side, though - there are not many people called Ingrid Emilia Williams".

He asked me to take a seat and try to be patient with him, but patience wasn't my virtue. I had sat in a hallway for over two hours waiting for an auntie and uncle to arrive who never appeared and asked repeatedly about my mother and father for over twelve years, always to be fobbed off. Whenever I had retaliated, I had been called an obnoxious, uncontrollable child.

The usher had returned, holding a huge book, which he placed on

CHAPTER TWELVE

a wooden pulpit. I had my fingers tightly crossed while I watched the other man turning the pages. After a long time, he asked the usher to get another book and again, watching him turning the pages repeatedly. I felt like a total nervous wreck. My heart was beating so fast.

Then, the gentleman looked at me, paused, and grinned.

"I have found your birth certificate" he said.

I went delirious with happiness. I waved my arms up high and, jumping up and down, gave the man a huge cuddle. Even the students downstairs were laughing and clapping. After twelve years I finally knew my mother's and father's names: Augustine Rose Williams and Alfred William Williams, whose job was a 'Confectioner'. The gentleman explained that to make sure, he had had to look at my parents' marriage certificate, and that was why it took so long.

When I eventually calmed down, I asked him if I had been adopted. He replied, "No, you were never adopted."

"How do you know that?" I said.

When the usher gave the birth certificate to the gentleman, he showed me the document and pointed out the empty box at the end.

"The empty box is for adopted parents' names only. Then you would be issued with a smaller version of your birth certificate. It's all government red tap to protect the real parents." I paid the fees and said all my good-byes. I couldn't thank the man enough.

Even with all the excitement, I did manage to find my way back. I had only one small hiccup getting on the right train, and sitting on that train I was so chuffed and my face was gleaming. I settled down for the journey, and it was only then that the penny dropped. Of course - the man who had made me candyfloss when I had gone for a day out with the Naylors that day. My father had been a confectioner.

I was dying to have a little peep every now and then and to tell everyone on the train what I had learned, but I didn't want everybody to think I was mad. 'They're coming to take me away, haha, heehee, hoho' as the song went.

When I got back to the hostel, I ran upstairs and jumped on my bed, kicking my legs up in the air. I was ecstatic over that piece of paper. This one piece of paper could transform my whole life, open doors which I had only dreamt of; finding my mother and father, and my files!

It took one day to find my birth certificate, yet it had taken the authorities ten years to find my real name. I'm not sure whether it was a miracle or fate, or whether it was an evil spirit with an alternative motive helping me that day.

When I heard Ruthie coming in, I ran downstairs and grabbed her. I practically dragged her upstairs and waved my birth certificate in her face. I even told her the story about my day out with the Naylors when I had been trapped in the toilets, and told her about the candyfloss man. Ruthie was so surprised and mystified with all I was telling her; it seemed so unbelievable.

In no time, the news had spread like wild fire. I told my fiancé and showed it to everyone at the hairdressers, but I had no intention of telling the Dooleys or Miss Knapman. I went about it in a sneaky way, because of the power they had over me.

The next day was Friday, and the hairdressers was packed. We had no time for idle gossip, which was in my favour, and when we had finished for the day, all that was on my mind was to get back to the hostel. When I got back, I ran straight upstairs to my room to look at my birth certificate. It had gone! I looked everywhere, my stomach churning over with rage. I asked everyone in that hostel if they had taken my birth certificate but they all said 'No'. One girl said, "I saw Miss Knapman leaving your room."

I went looking for the bitch, and bumped straight into her in the hallway. I asked her, not in a polite way, "May I have my birth certificate?"

CHAPTER TWELVE

"I don't know what you are talking about" she replied.

My blood was boiling, knowing she was lying to me. I asked her what she had been doing in my room, "One of the girls saw you leaving" she said. But she was ignoring me in a cunning way.

With all the commotion going on, Mr and Mrs Dooley came rushing down the stairs, demanding to know what was going on. When I told them, Mrs Dooley replied, "Yes, we have confiscated your birth certificate. You can have it back when you leave." I was like a bull in a china shop. I really wanted to smack her one, but she was a sick woman, so I turned my back on her and demanded that Miss Knapman give me back what belonged to me, including my money.

"I'll find my own place to live" I said.

All the girls had scarpered, and Mrs and Mr Dooley went into the office and closed the door. Miss Knapman pushed me to get by, which triggered me off. I retaliated by pushing her with all my might. In desperation, I ran towards the front door, but she pushed me in the back. I fell to the floor, then as soon as I got up she knocked me down again. I managed to scramble up and get one hand on the door handle, when Miss Knapman pushed me once more, so hard that I had to put my hands up to stop myself going through a pane of glass. In the end, I literally crawled out of that front door, and ran outside for my fiancé to pick me up in the car.

I stood there in the cold and rain, sobbing my heart out. Yet again I had been abused, violated, robbed of my identity. I did not know where to turn. I was beginning to wonder if I would ever be able to find myself and start living a normal life. I had come through so much, and yet I was still just a little girl lost.

To be continued

www.ingramcontent.com/pod-product-compliance
Lightning Source LLC
Chambersburg PA
CBHW061655040426
42446CB00010B/1756